American Proverbs
About Women

AMERICAN PROVERBS
ABOUT WOMEN

A Reference Guide

Lois Kerschen

Greenwood Press
Westport, Connecticut • London

Library of Congress Cataloging-in-Publication Data

Kerschen, Lois, 1951–
   American proverbs about women : a reference guide / Lois Kerschen.
     p. cm.
   Includes bibliographical references (p.   ) and index.
   ISBN 0–313–30442–4 (alk. paper)
    1. Proverbs, American—History and criticism.   2. Women—
Quotations, maxims, etc.   3. Women—Folklore.   4. Folklore—United
States.   I. Title.
PN6426.K47   1998
305.4—dc21   97–38580

British Library Cataloguing in Publication Data is available.

Library of Congress Catalog Card Number: 97–38580
ISBN: 0–313–30442–4

First published in 1998

Greenwood Press, 88 Post Road West, Westport, CT 06881
An imprint of Greenwood Publishing Group, Inc.

Printed in the United States of America

The paper used in this book complies with the
Permanent Paper Standard issued by the National
Information Standards Organization (Z39.48–1984).

10 9 8 7 6 5 4 3 2 1

Copyright Acknowledgment

Grateful acknowledgment is given for permission to quote from the following: *Women and
Language in Literature and Society*, Sally McConnell-Ginet, Ruth Borker, and Nelly Furman,
editors. Copyright © 1980 by Sally McConnell-Ginet, Ruth Borker, and Nelly Furman. Re-
produced with permission of Greenwood Publishing Group, Inc., Westport, CT.

CONTENTS

ACKNOWLEDGMENTS

There are a few people who deserve acknowledgment with the publication of this reference book. First are my uncle and aunt, Robert and Evelyn Kerschen Barnes. They are the only people who gave me true encouragement and helpful advice and tried to facilitate the production of this work. Their concern and aid, especially the persistent support of my aunt, will always be appreciated.

If it were not for the folklore class of the late Dr. Warren Walker, professor of English at Texas Tech University, I might not ever have discovered the joy of proverbs and then had the idea for this topic. For the kindness and cooperative suggestions that gave me a good start in pursuing this project, I am grateful to Dr. Walker.

This book might have remained a mere collection without the extent of analysis that I wanted to include had it not been for the freedom that my mentor, Dr. Fikre Tolossa, allowed me. Thanks to his gentle prodding, this work fleshed out tremendously and became recognizable scholarship.

One serendipity of this book is the excuse that it gave me to contact Dr. Wolfgang Mieder, the premier expert on proverbs and chair of the Department of German and Russian at the University of Vermont. Although I was a stranger to him, Dr. Mieder generously gave his time and offered invaluable advice concerning publication. The flowers that I sent to him when I got my book contract were well deserved.

Finally, I need to thank my husband, Stephen Ganus, for his computer expertise, his production assistance, his patience, and his loving faith in me. I couldn't have made it through all the trials and tribulations without him.

American Proverbs
About Women

INTRODUCTION

The title of this reference work, *American Proverbs About Women*, while seemingly simple, actually requires the discussion of a number of different areas in order to be understood. Before a collection of American proverbs about women can be presented, the broader category of folklore must be examined in terms of what it is and its historical relationship to women. Then it can be determined how proverbs are unique among folklore genres in their impact. From there, what is American and how American proverbs view women can be identified.

First of all, the subject of folklore as a whole should be considered. Often called the "voice of the folk," folklore is an oral tradition in songs, stories, myths, legends, riddles, rhymes, jokes, games, sayings, and more, but it is also dances, crafts, epitaphs, and the like. Folklore is the customs, beliefs, and practices of a people and, therefore, an expression of its culture. Jan Harold Brunvand, in *The Study of American Folklore: An Introduction*, said that folklore reveals "the common life of the human mind apart from what is contained in the formal records of culture that compose the heritage of a people."[1] As a result, folklore is an important indicator of a people's way of life and attitudes.

Until recent times, the study of folklore has largely excluded women. Whether this neglect resulted from the preponderance of male folklorists and anthropologists who failed to be sensitive to the possibility of another viewpoint or from the less personal but more pervasive bias of a male-dominated world, the consequence has been an invisibility of women in the picture of civilization's progress. Although the *Journal of American Folklore* published a bibliography of women's folklore as early as 1888, folklore scholarship pertaining to women has been minimal and, except for the areas of midwifery, charms, and some games, customs, and beliefs (premier folklorist Archer Taylor said, "If it could be seen from the kitchen window, it was woman's domain"[2]), women were not consulted by folklore field workers unless a male storyteller was unavailable. Consequently, a woman's unique form of expression and women's folk specialties, such as needlework and weaving, were left almost unrecorded until recent times. Now, however, with the rise of feminism, the search is on to find women's contributions in history and thereby give them their appropriate place.

Studies show not only how women have contributed, but also how they have been perceived through the ages. One of the functions of folklore is that of propaganda, as folklore is the perpetuation of tradition. The stories, proverbs, and other forms are a legacy of the customs, beliefs, and practices of one generation to the next. They are the embodiment of a way of life and all that it entails in terms of lessons and morals. Consequently, folklore stereotypes and presents roles in traditional forms for easy transmission. For Americans, this stereotyping has expressed itself both blatantly and subtly as patriarchy.

In his chapter "The Crowing Hen and the Easter Bunny: Male Chauvinism in American Folklore," noted folklore author Alan Dundes has provided the material for the following paraphrased list of American folklore characteristics concerning male-female images:

1. Boys are discussed first and discussed in terms of strength and largeness.

2. Girls are associated with sweet foodstuff, smallness, and a plaything nature.

3. Domestic servitude, as in homemaking and housekeeping, is defined for women.

4. Women are passive.

5. Women are expected to marry. The penalty for not doing so is to be the butt of cruel sayings and games about old maids.

6. The female path is that of love, marriage, and childbearing, not in careers like doctor, lawyer, Indian chief.

7. The female path does not include running amuck in Cupid's garden. Sex is a male prerogative maintained rigidly by a double standard. Women are victims of a man's right to sex. Boys sow wild oats while "nice girls blush."

8. Women are told what they should do, which is act like women, and what they should not do, which is act like men; thus the negative reactions to "tomboys" and "whistling girls."

9. Males are procreatively independent. The female procreative role is usurped by Santa, the stork, the Easter bunny, and others, thus limiting female activity.[3]

Exposing male chauvinism in most of folklore is a long process when one considers stories, legends, myths, songs, rhymes, and games. But the short pithy expressions that are proverbs make them easier to study as a group since their collection, while tedious, does not, however, require as much space as the other genres of folklore. Fortunately, the nature of proverbs is such that, while they are brief, they are perhaps the best indicators of attitudes and beliefs of any of the forms of folklore. Therefore, if one wants to explore the historical image of women in oral tradition, proverbs are an ideal subject.

Proverbs are difficult to define. While much has been written on what a proverb is, it is more important to understand what a proverb does. A proverb is a short homely statement that teaches a lesson or gives practical advice. There is generally a matter of rhyme and meter to consider and a binary structure that presents a problem in the first half and solves it in the second half. Usually, proverbs contain humor, but that humor, particularly when the subject is women, can be bitter, satirical, even macabre. Besides these typical proverbs, there are proverbial comparisons (As fussy as an old maid) that have a fixed traditional form but contain no moral advice; proverbial phrases (To smell like a whorehouse on Saturday night), which permit variations in person, number, and tense; proverbial similes (A man without a wife is like a fork without a knife); and proverbial metaphors (A widow is a boat without a rudder). All of these forms capsulize an everyday experience, both of the originator of the proverb and of the one who uses it.

Concerning origins, those to whom credit is given for coining certain proverbs are probably still not the authors. Proverbs have been documented back to the time of Aristotle and Plato, and can be found as rules of conduct in the most primitive societies. It is this latter fact that leads us into consideration of the importance of proverbs and of their function within a culture.

"Proverbs being drawn from the experiences and study of a people's lives are among the most accurate index of that people's life and thought. They may not be true or represent truth, but they indicate what the people hold to as their rules and ideals of life and conduct." So wrote Joyce Hertzler in "The Social Wisdom of the Primitives with Special Reference to Their Proverbs." Hertzler concluded that proverbs more accurately represent a people's rules and ideals than their religious or ethical systems.[4] Appropriately published in a periodical entitled *Social Forces*, these remarks by Hertzler strongly make the point that proverbs are not just fun retorts, but are an important medium for teaching and learning. Yet there are no high moral ideas expressed in proverbs, only practical ways to survive in the real world.

Further proof of the impact of proverbs can be found in what Charlotte Sophia Burne wrote in *The Handbook of Folklore*: "The morality of a people, what they think is good or evil, what they advise and what they condemn, who is respectable and whose conduct is unacceptable, this can be found in their proverbs and popular sayings."[5] While Hertzler thought that modern society should be too complex for proverbs because our problems are not so simple that they can be covered by a pat saying, what should be and what is are once again in conflict. Admittedly, Hertzler was correct when she said that proverbs "take away the necessity of individual generalization and explanation. They reduce the demand for accurate observation and analysis and for correct expression. Those who use proverbs extensively have their thoughts both guided and confined by them."[6] Therefore, Hertzler concluded, educated people do not need them, and to use proverbs is to return to the primitive, illiterate state. Nonetheless, don't people, even the best educated, tend to reach for their grab bag of clichés rather than think of something original to say when a response is required?

Proverbs provide, then, an ease of communication. They are handed down as useful "saws," tried and, people are told, true expressions that can handle any situation. Such verbal tools have long been popular and continue to be so. During the height of their popularity in the 1600s and 1700s when many collections were made, proverbs were considered not the resource of the primitive and illiterate, but "dear to the true intellectual aristocracy of a nation."[7] This latter judgment was made in 1859 by Richard Chenevix Trench, Archbishop of Dublin, who worried in his book, *Proverbs and their Lessons*, that people are "very little conscious of the amusement, instruction, insight, which they are capable of yielding."[8] Apparently, American authors were aware of the weight of proverbs because, in the period of 1820–1880, proverbs abound. Consequently, Archer Taylor and Bartlett Jere Whiting chose 1820–1880 as the years to study for their *Dictionary of American Proverbs and Proverbial Phrases* for "at no other time have so many American writers made proverbs so obvious an ingredient in their style."[9]

Sixty years after this literary era of heavy proverbial use, Roger L. Welsch wrote in *A Treasury of Nebraska Pioneer Folklore* that proverbs were as common then as three generations before. Welsch found it astonishing how frequently proverbs appeared in everyday conversation: "When someone wants to make a comparison, or needs to prove a point, or sees a red sunset, time and again he [*sic*] will find himself [*sic*] phrasing his [*sic*] comments in terms of a folk saying, proverb or prophecy."[10]

Because of this widespread knowledge and dissemination of proverbs and their importance as indicators of societal norms, modern psychologists use proverbs as part of their diagnostic testing material. Proverbs have been used to test for personality traits, attitude, schizophrenia, depression, abstracting function, cerebral disease, and cognition.

Psychologists should not be the only ones to use proverbs to gain insight into the human mind. For example, for anthropologists and sociologists, proverbs can be seen as a tool of the patriarchy established at the beginning of humanity when the caveman's physical prowess, essential to survival as a hunter and protector, caused him to think that he was superior to the cavewoman. Through the centuries, this preference for brawn instead of brain has given the world a violent history and a patriarchy that codified male dominance into law from the Bible to the Napoleonic Code. As part of the process, the proverb has been used to translate this biased law into lay terms.

For the folklorist, the student of literature, and the linguist interested in the ethnic and sexist bias of language, the proverb can also provide many answers. One is what one says, so our language trains us and betrays us. Peter Seitel, in "Proverbs: A Social Use of Metaphor," said that, for folklorists, the study of proverbs can be as "white rats are to experimental psychologists and as kinship terms are to cultural anthropologists . . . by pushing around these small and apparently simply constructed items, one can discover principles which give order to a wider range of phenomena. Proverbs are the simplest of the metaphorical genres of folklore . . . and the genre which clearly and directly is used to serve a social purpose."[11] What Seitel is indicating is that, through the study of proverbs, one can understand the more complex genres of folklore and gain significant insight into the social purposes that literature of all kinds may serve. Despite being a relatively simple application of metaphor, since proverbs are, according to Seitel, the "most sensitive to social context,"[12] if one can master the numerous and complex social rules to use and interpret proverbs, then the rest is easy.

The worthwhile pursuit of studying proverbs, then, can determine whether or not ancient ideals influence current American thought. If so, then the question becomes: Are these positive or relevant influences? The investigation of the origins of proverbs may reveal prejudices and mores that are no longer congruent with our modern mentality and therefore should be gleaned from our teachings. Joseph Raymond's article "Tension in Proverbs" illustrates this problem. Raymond added to the proverb's definition as a vivid expression of group mind, memory, and feelings, the elements of volition and tension. He pointed out that certain groups are "proverbially rejected for economic, ethnic, religious, regional or other reasons" [including gender] and that these groups constitute significant material for social study. Raymond noted that derogatory statements frequently are in proverb form and that some proverbial phrases may be clues to historical tensions "whose currency, extensiveness, weighting in the culture, and contextual definition would have to be established before tentative conclusions could be drawn as to types of existing tensions. When such phrases are particularly pungent, they may outlast the circumstances which popularized them."[13]

This book will expose some of the existing tensions in American proverbs about women and suggest that some of these proverbs have out-
lasted the circumstances that popularized them. In the process, we
should note Alan Dundes' reminder that we cannot censor folklore, for
we must treat the disease of prejudice, not the symptoms. But we must
also point out the symptoms as often as possible. Since "the male bias
in American culture is not just reflected passively in American folklore"
but is "actively transmitted to each new generation of Americans, often
unconsciously or unselfconsciously through folkloristic means," then by
"making the unconscious or unselfconscious conscious, we may raise
levels of consciousness. We cannot stop folklore, but we can hold it up
to the light of reason and through the unrivaled picture it provides, we
may better see what wrongs need righting."[14]

While the majority of proverbs are sexless in subject, those that deal
with women tend to fall into certain patterns, and the collection that
follows will divide the proverbs into these categories. Generally speaking,
proverbs about women are characterized by biting wit and bitter complaints. While some proverbs are the saccharine, "up on a pedestal" kind
(God couldn't be everywhere; therefore, He made mothers), the majority
portray woman as a sharp-tongued, long-winded, empty-headed, toylike
creature who is faithless to the man by whom she should be ruled and
to whom she belongs like property or livestock.

Proverbs stereotype without shame, yet contradict each other constantly. For every proverb that promotes the submissiveness of women,
there is another that admits that women will not always accept a subor-
dinate position but will find a way around it. "However, the very existence of such contradictory statements about women indicates that what
they say and do has had some impact on how men run their lives.
Women's activities cannot be easily forecast, men complain. Women cannot be totally ignored even if (or especially because) their behavior often
seems to men to be idiosyncratic and illogical rather than carefully
planned."[15] So adds Cheris Kramarae in *Women and Men Speaking*. The
problem here might be that women will, of course, appear to be bizarre
and confusing if their roles are defined on the basis of men's attitudes.
Woman, as an aberration in a man's world, constitutes a separate category
for proverbs, while there is not a similar set of sayings about men, since
everything is observed from their point of view. There need not be proverbs that chide subtle assumptions of power by men because their authority is obvious and considered natural.

Logic suggests that women have seldom originated proverbs since men
have dominated literature and society historically. Supporting this theory
is evidence from a related case. Archer Taylor remarked in *The Proverb
and an Index to the Proverb* that the Wellerism, a cousin to the proverb
that incongruously combines a sober assertion with an utterly inappro-

priate scene (Everyone to his own taste, as the old lady said when she kissed the cow), displays a freedom and scant respect "toward women, particularly old women," which shows that "the form is a masculine invention in which women have had little share."[16]

What we know of the power of language also suggests that men have used every form of expression to vent their fears, jealousies, and misconceptions about women. Tristram Potter Coffin, a leading folklorist, commented in his book, *Our Living Traditions: An Introduction to American Folklore*, about this retribution: "One of the richest sources of proverbs is [a] man's fears and hatreds of his fellow man, his xenophobia. [A] Man is always willing, even eager, to characterize, deride, spoof his fellow man, especially if in doing so he thinks he is raising himself in the eyes of the world or in his own. In such proverbs there are of course numerous example's of [a] man's earliest objects of derision, women—anti-feminism, fear and hatred of women, especially wives."[17]

The problem with this behavior is that such speech, disguised as "the wisdom of many, the wit of one" (the traditional definition of a proverb), buys its wit and retribution at the expense of others. Besides the moral, there is the consequence to consider. The quick repartee may not seem to matter much at first glance, but, as pointed out many times, folklore is much more than the recording of quaint customs—it is a perpetuator of attitudes and values. As a living organism permeating American life, folklore is accepted without thought just as any other form of propaganda. Subliminal cuts are dangerous: so short and unobtrusive that they slip into our subconscious and program our thinking without our ever knowing the source. After all, how many times can one hear "Hell hath no fury like a woman scorned" before one believes that women truly are vicious and vindictive? Like so many matters of faith or status quo, one does not question but simply accepts that that is just the way it is.

The very familiarity of proverbs begs acceptance and trust, but folklore scholars today are questioning the appropriateness of the proverbs' messages. The new interest in women's issues has prompted an examination of the treatment of women by folklore and, in the case of this book, particularly by proverbs. The attitude toward women, shared by both men and women, may have been formed by proverbs, which has resulted in men maintaining superiority and women accepting subordination and ridicule, despite modern enlightenment. The confusion that results has been a primary topic of American society for the last quarter century. It is reasoned that women are capable enough to be business leaders, for example, yet women's salaries fall far below men's and a glass ceiling keeps women out of high-level positions.

It is appropriate at this point to review the importance of examining proverbs for the purpose of determining their influence on the status of women. In "Problems in the Study of Proverbs," Archer Taylor drives home some important thoughts about how the historical and stylistic investigation of proverbs, and therewith of cultural roots, exposes our current values. Chance did not determine the course of history. Powerful influences have shaped world events and are reflected in the development of a phrase. Thus, a "simple turn of speech lets us view civilization from a mountain peak." Value, however, "comes only from interpreting the facts to meet our cultural needs or to feed our spirits. The interpretation may be in terms of history, cultural history, aesthetic standards, or, in short, any social activity. The fact is necessary and equally so the interpretation."[18]

If what proverbs teach isn't examined to find what Americans really believe, the culture will continue to harbor resentment, misunderstanding, and prejudice concerning women. Thus the battle of the sexes will rage on with no victors, only victims.

BACKGROUND STUDY

Since publications rather than field work were used for the sources of the proverbs in this reference book, a review of proverb collections was, of course, necessary. These collections will be discussed in the following section. Besides the proverbs themselves, though, it was necessary to review many other works about folklore and the study of proverbs in order to understand the field and the particular area of concern about women.

Jan Harold Brunvand's *The Study of American Folklore* provided the definitions used and a beginning bibliography. Richard M. Dorson's *American Folklore* provided the following food for thought while searching for supporting material for the working premise about women and American proverbs: Folklore is linked to nationalistic pride and can be used as propaganda; American folklore must be seen against the background of American history; American folklore is a blend of European and Native American folklore; there are three themes for American folklore: land, savages, and hazards of life; and, the proverb is the very "bone and sinew" of the Pennsylvania Dutch dialect.[19]

Similarly, Kaarle Krohn's *Folklore Methodology* teaches that a proverb is a prediction based on true experience that has attained a crystallized form, that is, it crystallizes life's experiences. "The true proverb . . . frequently contains a concept that gives color and life to the linguistic expression of the idea." In addition, Krohn reports that Fr. Seiler says in *Das deutsche Sprichwort* (Strassburg, 1918, p. 8), "In the creation of a proverb, just as in the fashioning of a single word or expression, the folk exercise is not a creative but rather a selective function."[20]

Another well-known authority on folklore, Richard M. Dorson, wrote in *Folklore and Folklife: An Introduction* that "Proverbs are one of the most easily observed and collected genres of traditional expression, yet one of the least understood. This misunderstanding is due, perhaps, to their very familiarity." Dorson provided some discussion of the long history of proverb collections in print and said that "In fact, many of the earliest and most popular of books were collections of proverbs, the most notable being Erasmus's best seller of the early Renaissance, the *Copia*." He added that proverb collecting has primarily been done in encyclopedic form "and with a great deal of borrowing from one compilation to the next."[21] This last bit of information is certainly true, and this repetition can be seen in the index where one proverb may have several sources cited.

Many of the books and articles on folklore and proverbs that I consulted gave valuable definitions of a proverb (the lengthy explanation of proverbs and related forms in the *Standard Dictionary of Folklore, Mythology and Legend* edited by Maria Leach is excellent). But verification of the power and influence of a proverb, and justification of the project and the belief that proverbs can influence attitudes, was also sought. Support was found in a premier authority on proverbs, Archer Taylor, who said in "Problems in the Study of Proverbs" that through proverbs "We are led very directly to estimate the worth of different manners of expression and to perceive currents of ideas—ethical, political, scientific, or aesthetic—in the history of humanity." He added: "The survey of the origin and dissemination of a proverb, the critical and appreciative judgment of its various forms, the examination of the way it has been used, or the interpretation of a misunderstood proverb are tasks which repay amply the comparatively slight effort needed to accomplish them."[22]

Donald R. Gorham's "A Proverbs Test for Clinical and Experimental Use," which said that "proverbs have long been used as an index of intellectual functioning" (e.g., the Stanford-Binet Intelligence Scale),[23] and "Use of Meaningless and Novel Proverbs as a Projective Technique" by Larry W. Bailey and Darrel Edwards, both provided evidence of the psychological impact of proverbs. In fact, Bailey and Edwards said that

> Proverbs have been used for many years and in widely dispersed cultures as a means of conveying basic truths which have emerged from man's experience. Proverbs characteristically involve an element of interest and intrigue, symbolism, and general application of principle. Because of this figurativeness and lack of specificity of concepts, translation and application of the proverb are left to the interpreter. Thus, proverbs have frequently been used to assess abstract thinking, level of verbal understanding, and personality factors. . . . That interpretations of proverbs may provide rich qualitative material reflecting the interpreter's dynamics and life in many instances the interpreter will project his needs, attitudes and conflicts into his responses.[24]

One of the greatest aids to this project was *American Proverb Literature: A Bibliography* compiled by Francis A. DeCaro and W. K. McNeil.
This annotated bibliography saved many hours of searching for sources
and guides by providing not only a list of works in folklore, but also a
critique of their value. Sometimes just the note on the work was enough
to determine its value in connection with the subject of this reference
book and to stimulate further thought on it. For example, concerning
Alexander H. Krappe's chapter on proverbs in *The Science of Folklore*
they wrote: "This chapter notes certain problems encountered in dealing
with proverbs. [e.g.] The fact that contradictory proverbs can be found
in the same culture is accounted for by the fact that common sense as a
whole warns against all excesses or extremes. . . . This last proposition of
Krappe is an interesting one, but it would seem that contradictory proverbs can be accounted for without resorting to the mystique of a sort of
collective folk mind which in the end puts all into harmony."[25]

The length of the bibliography is an indication of the extent of the
research done into the discussion of proverbs by folklorists. It was necessary, of course, to find out if anyone else had approached American
proverbs from the angle of their treatment of women or had studied
other elements of folklore in such terms. Support was found for the
premise of this book, but nothing else was found exactly like this reference work. In fact, discussions with researchers at two of the largest
women's studies centers in the nation, the Henry A. Murray Research
Center at Radcliffe College of Harvard University and the National
Women's Studies Association at the University of Maryland, revealed that
they had no knowledge of anything similar to this work.

T. F. Thiselton-Dyer's *Folklore of Women*, published in Chicago in
1906, is on the same topic, but it contains proverbs from all over the
world. The discussion in this book is mostly historical, but because of
that aspect, it was possible to identify the origins of many proverbs about
women and to get explanations of their meanings.

There have been four books on the market in recent years that are
vaguely similar in nature to this work. *The Monstrous Regiment* by Margaret Blackwood is a book of aphorisms about women published in England in 1990. The book is divided into categories much like this one, and
the sayings from various famous people throughout history are also very
revealing of attitudes toward women.

An Uncommon Scold by Abby Adams contains 1,000 quotes from famous women. This book is also divided into categories, that is, topics
about which women have expressed their views through the centuries,
but there is only one section on the subject of women themselves. Another book quoting women is *Wit and Wisdom of Famous American
Women* edited by Evelyn L. Beilenson and Ann L. Tenenbaum. This very
small book (the others were not large by any means) is restricted to an

American focus, like this work, but is divided according to the occupa-
tions of the women quoted. Finally, there is another very small book
Momilies: As My Mother Used to Say . . . by Michele Slung. This bestseller
is a collection of the things that mothers say with pictures of mothers of
many famous people.

While these four books are also concerned with women and sayings,
none are collections of proverbs and little is actually said about the impact of language on society as it deals with women. Among the proverb
collections, almost all are general in nature. They have women, daughters, wives, and so forth, as subject headings, but there is no gathering
of these related groups for the purpose of discussing traits or trends,
impact or significance. Nearly all the collections have some discussion in
their prefaces concerning the nature of proverbs, their structure, popularity, history, and international similarities, but it is rare to find any de-
tailed analysis of a select group of proverbs.

Articles about proverbs usually present the latest collections from a
particular area of the country. Although dozens were reviewed, not many
of these articles actually contributed new proverbs to this collection since
they could be about any topic and didn't often have one that concerned
women. It must be remembered that, out of the thousands of proverbs
that have been recorded, those about women are a relatively small per-
centage even if they are in the hundreds.

Because of the aforementioned general nature of proverb collections
and the lack of discussion about the impact of the proverbs as part of
our language, it was necessary to look at the arena of linguistics to get
reinforcement of the idea that language is a powerful tool and that any
given segment of language can have a key influence on a culture and its
thought patterns. The link to linguistics was, of course, the study of sexist
language. Proverbs about women are a worry because they appear to be
laden with sexism. So, as a part of language, proverbs about women are,
in particular, a part of sexist language just as much as the generic pronoun. The following is a quick overview of what was found to be useful
from the world of linguistics.

There were a multitude of books and articles about sexism in language
to call upon, but most, in particular the works of Deborah Tannen, dealt
with the way women speak, the way women are spoken to, interactions
in conversation between the sexes, word endings like "-ette" and "-ess,"
negative connotations for "feminine" traits while "masculine" descrip-
tions are positive, and other well-known topics in the discussion of sexist
language. Nonetheless, the point was made by many researchers that language in all its forms of usage has a definite influence on a society's
thinking. The argument was the same in linguistics as it is in folklore:
How much does language affect a culture versus how much does a culture affect the language?

"Determinism" is a school of thought championed among linguists by Dale Spender who wrote *Man Made Language* in 1980. According to Deborah Cameron in *Feminism and Linguistic Theory*, Dale Spender and other feminist writers, by the end of the 1970s, were proponents of the theory that language strongly affects and maybe even determines one's view of the world. Cameron herself discussed the "images" that are imprinted on our minds about women from representations in beauty pageants, advertising, literature, children's books, and so on.[26] If the representation of women in these images is of concern, why not also how women are represented in proverbs?

Women and Language in Literature and Society, edited by Sally McConnell-Ginet, Ruth Borker, and Nelly Furman, provided some interesting selections that dealt not only with parts of the language, but also with the force of language as a whole in teaching women about their place. In their introduction, the editors said that "research suggests the importance of linguistic *processes* in connecting individual human minds in a larger sociopolitical order. It also points to the important issue of how product and process, language structure and language use, interact with one another."[27] Continuing this line of thought, Philip M. Smith said in *Language, The Sexes and Society* that "There is more to this domain of activity than the interest in language as a social telltale, however. This is the concern that language, as a major vehicle for the transmission of beliefs and values of society, may profoundly *affect* female-male relations."[28]

If this effect exists, can it be seen in everyday life, for example, in the workplace? Probably so, but studies to verify proverb use in the home or in the office or in social situations are virtually nonexistent. Neal R. Norrick in *How Proverbs Mean: Semantic Studies in English Proverbs* reported that "Recordings and/or transcriptions of naturally occurring dialogue have been practically inaccessible until recently and they remain rare . . . a systematic investigation of proverbs in free conversation would require more recorded or transcribed conversations than are at present available and the long-term efforts of a research team."[29]

Consequently, the contention that proverbs about women affect how they are treated in everyday life cannot be supported through the literature. It can only be said that the evidence to date leads logically to such a conclusion. Nonetheless, some testimony has been gathered from the experiences of women in the workplace regarding language, if not proverbs themselves. *Words and Women* by Casey Miller and Kate Swift provided help in this area as well as other important reading about women, language, and society.

Since all subjects are in one way or another interdisciplinary, besides linguistics, material from anthropology and psychology is listed in the bibliography. Anthropologists have often written about the importance of the proverb in primitive societies, indeed in all societies, as a pocket-size description or snapshot of a culture. The link with psychology has already been established, but Kenneth L. Dion's article "Psychology and Proverbs," which emphatically encourages psychologists to study proverbs because they "seem to focus on fundamental values in a given society and reflect important aspects of the human condition," supports the reasoning used when I included countries of origin with the lists of proverbs in this collection. Dion said that the dictionaries of proverbs that list the historical period when the proverb emerged, permitting historical comparisons within and between cultures, show "Commonalities of proverbs across cultures and across time . . . reflecting more generalized human concerns as well as cultural diffusion over time of proverbial wisdom."[30]

In reviewing literature for this reference book, an effort was made to reach as much material as possible. Computer databases and interlibrary loans helped enormously. Also consulted were the women's studies and gender sources on the Internet, which had links to more bibliographies than it was humanly possible to check. However, the library holdings of the Henry A. Murray Research Center of Radcliffe College of Harvard University, a leading repository of women's studies material, were accessed, as well as the Indiana University Folklore Library on-line. A senior researcher at the Murray Center said that she had never before had a request for this type of information and that she didn't know where to find something about it. A librarian at Indiana University reviewed the bibliography and said that it seemed to her that all of the folklore material that would be pertinent to this work had been found. Thus it appears that exhaustive research on an original topic has been accomplished with this reference book.

METHOD AND PRESENTATION

America, the land of the immigrants and all they brought with them, was thought not to have a literature of its own until the nineteenth century. American writers in the seventeenth century wrote travel literature, histories, and diaries—choices befitting a people trying to record the great adventure of colonizing the New World. Although there was some poetry from the beginning, American writers into the eighteenth century were not pursuing literature as an art, but rather were religious and political leaders who produced practical essays for the edification of others and continued to provide records of the American experience. Eventually, satires, short moralistic tales, and even a few novels and plays appeared. Finally, in the nineteenth century, there were those who made their living at writing and produced classic examples of belles-lettres in the form of fiction and poetry as well as dialect humor and local-color stories. European acceptance of the idea of an American literature did not come readily, but the enormous popularity of the unique American story and the quality of the writing could not be denied. American writers gained recognition throughout the world, and a true American literary tradition was born.

Proverbs, however, are hard to identify as uniquely American because so many were continuations of proverbs from "the old country." Wolfgang Mieder, Stewart Kingsley, and Kelsie Harder, the editors of *A Dictionary of American Proverbs*, published in 1992, addressed the question of what makes a proverb particularly "American" in their introduction. Their answer was that a proverb can be classified as American if it is in common use in North America or, of course, if it originated here. The same parameters are used here, although limited to the United States. While it is technically incorrect to call "American" those things that are from the United States of America only as opposed to those things that come from any of the Americas (North, Central, and South), all of the U.S. collections reviewed for this book called themselves American, so this common practice is followed here. Another difference with Mieder, Kingsley, and Harder is that they gathered their proverbs from forty years of field work by the American Dialect Society, but for this book the sources were already published collections of proverbs that identified those proverbs that were considered American. After all, the intent was not to collect anew, but to examine for trends what has already been collected in one subject area.

While journal articles provided a number of the proverbs in this collection (though perhaps only one or a few at a time), the majority came from the following books that each contributed twenty-five or many more:

> *Dictionary of American Proverbs*, David Kin, editor, 1955
>
> *A Dictionary of American Proverbs*, Wolfgang Mieder, editor in chief, 1992
>
> *A Dictionary of American Proverbs and Proverbial Phrases, 1820–1880*, Archer Taylor and Bartlett Jere Whiting, 1958
>
> *Early American Proverbs and Proverbial Phrases*, Bartlett Jere Whiting, 1977
>
> *Frontier Folksay: Proverbial Lore of the Inland Pacific Northwest Frontier*, Donald M. Hines, 1977
>
> *Modern Proverbs and Proverbial Sayings*, Bartlett Jere Whiting, 1989
>
> "Proverbs and Proverbial Sayings" in the *Frank C. Brown Collection of North Carolina Folklore*, vol. 1, Bartlett Jere Whiting, 1952
>
> *Talk Less and Say More: Vermont Proverbs*, Wolfgang Mieder, 1986

Raymond Lamont Brown's book, *A Book of Proverbs*, ultimately contributed over fifty proverbs, but it is a classic example of the difficulty of choosing the proverbs for an American collection. Brown's book was published in New York in 1970. It is an American book, but careful reading reveals that the proverbs presented are actually from around the world. Only in certain areas were the proverbs clearly identified as American, and those were ones that originated in the States. However, Brown is given credit for those proverbs about women found in his book that were verified as in use in the United States through other sources.

Two articles by Grant C. Loomis for *Western Folklore* supplied a notable number of proverbs: "Proverbs in the Golden Era" (1955) and "Proverbs in the Farmer's Almanac(k)," (1956). Speaking of almanacs, a collection of American proverbs would not be complete without the inclusion of those from Benjamin Franklin's *Poor Richard's Almanack*, and many are referenced in this work. It should be noted that collections from across the country are represented: California, Indiana, New Mexico, New York (Thompson), North Carolina, Texas, Vermont, and Washington (Person).

One important difference between this collection and some others, most notably the Mieder dictionary, is that some published only true proverbs while included here are some phrases, sayings, and proverbial comparisons, especially those found by Taylor and Whiting.

Not included are any sayings that happened to contain words like "mother" or "daughter" (Necessity is the mother of invention; Admiration is the daughter of ignorance), but did not really describe women or make a comment about them. There were also some proverbs that offer marital advice to women, but again they do not give an insight into society's view of women; they only address women.

A number of standard and foreign collections were reviewed in search of origins for American counterparts. Of course, many of the American books and articles used for this collection gave the country of origin for the proverb already listed. As a result, when the country of origin is known, it is listed in both the category section and the Alphabetical Index because it is interesting to look for trends that might be discerned in different cultures. The same is true for different geographical areas of the United States. In particular, proverbs from the southwestern portion of the country seem to stand out for their manner of expression.

The organization of this reference book is as follows. First, the proverbs identified as American are presented in categories. These categories were chosen according to the natural patterns into which the proverbs seemed to fall, that is, according to the type of message they carry. Since the topic is women, some groupings were obvious identifications such as mothers or situations such as married and widowed, while others describe women in a certain way, such as virtuous or as property. While these categories are arbitrary and could have been chosen differently, it is interesting to note that T. F. Thiselton-Dyer used virtually the same divisions in his book *Folklore of Women*.

In the category section, the proverbs are presented in alphabetical order with any variations, any references to like proverbs, any year of first-known publication information, the nationality of the proverb's origin if that is known (or at least where is it also known to be used), or the name of any state where the proverb is known to be used. Bibliographic information is not included. The date of first-known publication is provided because it makes another interesting reference point for analysis. Information in brackets is the author's. Proverbs are cited as written in the source, so readers will find the generic pronoun used—another indication of sexism in language.

The proverbs are preceded in each chapter by an interpretive introduction. In the shorter chapters, an effort was made to include a discussion of every proverb from that category in the introduction, but in the larger chapters, not every proverb could be included without getting ridiculously long and repetitive. Besides, the reader should be allowed to have some sense of self-discovery, so representative samples should be sufficient to point out trends and the controversial and intriguing messages.

Also, the format is arranged so as to list the proverbs one at a time to make it easy to distinguish one from another. The biggest problem with Thiselton-Dyer's book was that the material was presented in paragraph form, so it was impossible to find any one particular proverb without reading through a mass of prose. This effort to separate information into clearly distinguishable parts took a great deal of time and space, but it is similar to the dictionary form that one finds in other collections.

The categories appear in order of the largest group of proverbs to the smallest group, followed by a miscellaneous section. These selections are by no means definitive—many proverbs could have fit into more than one category; they are only an attempt to organize the collection into a workable scheme.

A conclusion regarding the implications of the collection is given as the last chapter. Suggestions for further study and a review of the questions raised by this collection are discussed there.

Following the chapters, there is an Alphabetical Index of Proverbs. In this section, the source of the proverb, whether in one publication or more, will be listed, and the page number for the place of the proverb in a category chapter will be given. Once again, variations, state, nationality, and year of first-known publication information will be provided.

A Bibliography is given citing first the many sources for the proverbs found in books and then periodicals, and listing second the scholarly works about proverbs, women's studies, linguistics, and other areas related to this study that were consulted, also divided between books and periodicals.

Finally, a general Index cites information from the Introduction and introductory sections to each of the chapters.

NOTES

1. Jan Harold Brunvand, *The Study of American Folklore: An Introduction*, 2nd ed. (New York: W. W. Norton and Co., Inc., 1978), 1.

2. Claire R. Farrer, "Women and Folklore: Images and Genres," *Journal of American Folklore* 88 (Jan.-Mar. 1975): xi.

3. Alan Dundes, "The Crowing Hen and the Easter Bunny: Male Chauvinism in American Folklore," *Interpreting Folklore* (Bloomington: Indiana University Press, 1980), 161–65, 170.

4. Joyce Hertzler, "The Social Wisdom of the Primitives with Special Reference to Their Proverbs," *Social Forces* 11 (1933): 315.

5. Charlotte Sophia Burne, *The Handbook of Folklore* (London: Sidgwick and Jackson, Ltd., 1914), 280.

6. Hertzler, "Social Wisdom," 317.

7. Richard Chenevix Trench, *Proverbs and their Lessons* (New York: E. P. Dutton and Co., 1905), 11.

8. Ibid., 9–10.

9. Archer Taylor and Bartlett Jere Whiting, *A Dictionary of American Proverbs and Proverbial Phrases, 1820–1880* (Cambridge, MA: The Belknap Press of Harvard University Press, 1958), viii.

10. Roger L. Welsch, *A Treasury of Nebraska Pioneer Folklore* (Lincoln: University of Nebraska Press, 1941), 266.

11. Peter Seitel, "Proverbs: A Social Use of Metaphor," *Genre* 2 (1969): 159.

12. Ibid.

13. Joseph Raymond, "Tension in Proverbs: More Light on International Understanding," *Western Folklore* 15 (1956): 155–56.

14. Dundes, "Crowing Hen," 160, 175.

15. Cheris Kramarae, *Women and Men Speaking: Frameworks for Analysis* (Rowley, MA: Newbury House Publishers, Inc., 1981), 122.

16. Archer Taylor, *The Proverb and an Index to the Proverb* (Hatboro, PA: Folklore Associates, 1962), 217.

17. Tristram Potter Coffin, ed., *Our Living Traditions: An Introduction to American Folklore* (New York: Basic Books, 1968), 201.

18. Archer Taylor, "Problems in the Study of Proverbs," *Journal of American Folklore* 47 (1934): 21.

19. Richard M. Dorson, *American Folklore* (Chicago: The University of Chicago Press, 1959), 3, 5, 7, 9, 78.

20. Kaarle Krohn, *Folklore Methodology*, trans. Roger L. Welsch (Austin: University of Texas Press, 1971), 23, 24, 25.

21. Richard M. Dorson, ed., *Folklore and Folklife: An Introduction* (Chicago: The University of Chicago Press, 1972), 117–18.

22. Taylor, "Problems," 1, 10.

23. Donald R. Gorham, "A Proverbs Test for Clinical and Experimental Use," *Psychological Reports* 2 (1956): 1.

24. Larry W. Bailey and David Edwards, "Use of Meaningless and Novel Prov-

erbs as a Projective Technique," *Journal of Personality Assessment* 37 (1973): 527.

    25. Francis A. DeCaro and W. K. McNeil, comps., *American Proverb Literature: A Bibliography*, Bibliographic and Special Series, No. 6 (Bloomington, IN: Folklore Forum, 1970), 5.

    26. Deborah Cameron, *Feminism and Linguistic Theory* (1985; New York: St. Martin's Press, 1992), 5–6.

    27. Sally McConnell-Ginet, Ruth Borker, and Nelly Furman, eds., *Women and Language in Literature and Society* (New York: Praeger, 1980), 5.

    28. Philip M. Smith, *Language, The Sexes and Society* (New York: Basil Blackwell Inc., 1985), 13.

    29. Neal R. Norrick, *How Proverbs Mean: Semantic Studies in English Proverbs* (New York: Mouton Publishers, 1985), 6.

    30. Kenneth L. Dion, "Psychology and Proverbs," *Canadian Psychology* 31.3 (1990): 210.

1

WIVES AND MARRIAGE

The overwhelming majority of proverbs that discuss women in a role deal with women as wives (A wife is a young man's slave and an old man's darling) or the subject of marriage as it affects women (Marriage is the supreme blunder that all women make). A whole spectrum of attitudes is reflected in these proverbs: advice, warnings, overt double standards, appreciation, and resignation.

The opening proverb below, "All are good girls, but where do the bad wives come from?" (see also: A good maid sometimes makes a bad wife), begins the discussion where all marriages begin—two people are in love and expect that they will live happily ever after. But "All married women are not wives," and "Lots of men get women, but few get wives." In fact, "The most fascinating women never make the best marriages."

But who makes a good marriage? Is it "A good wife is the workmanship of a good husband" or "A good wife makes a good husband"? One proverb says "The happiest wife is not she that gets the best husband but she that makes the best of that which she gets." But what if "She drove her ducks to a poor market," that is, she made a bad marriage from the start? Then, "She that hath a bad husband hath a hell within her own house," and she "shows it in her dress." (Concerning this latter expression, Thiselton-Dyer explained that "the wife who has a grievance will be sure to make it known."[1]) Indeed, "If you want to know a bad husband, look at his wife's countenance."

Although there is a proverb that says "One good husband is worth two good wives; for the scarcer things are the more they're valued," the proverb makers lean more to the belief that it is the wife who causes the most problems within a marriage. Starting with the attitude that "Matrimony is an insane idea on the part of a man to pay some woman's board" and "When a man takes a wife, he ceases to dread hell," it is no wonder that men are advised "When you choose a wife shut your eyes and commend your soul to God." Should a man get a bad wife, he will have "purgatory for a neighbor." In fact, he will quickly come to know that there are only "Two good days for a man in his life: when he weds, and when he buries his wife" and that "A wife is seen with pleasure only at the wedding and in the winding sheet." This thought continues in two other proverbs: "Grief for a dead wife, and a troublesome guest, continues to the threshold and there is at rest. But I mean such wives as are none of the best" and "It's a sweet sorrow to bury a nagging wife."

Since money is so important to men, it is no surprise that one of their major complaints against their wives is the expense of being married (It is cheaper to find a wife than to feed a wife). So, first, one should marry money: "A fair wife without a fortune is a fine house without furniture." Once married, "Many a man sees a wolf at the door because his wife sees a mink in the window" and "A nice wife and a back door oft do make a rich man poor." Or so he says. "Generally when a man feels the need for economy he thinks it ought to begin with his wife" because "Many blame the wife for their own thriftless life." So he tells her, "Wife, make thine own candle, Spare penny to handle."

Trusting a wife seems to be another big problem for men: "Give your wife the short knife, keep the long one yourself." A man shouldn't confide in his wife: "He knows little who tells his wife all he knows"; "He that tells his wife news is but newly married." Also, "He who loves his wife should watch her," and that is why "God is the guardian of a blind man's wife" because, as Thiselton-Dyer explained, the blind man "cannot look after her and control her movements."[2] Of course, if a man marries a beautiful woman he is just asking for trouble: "He that hath a fair wife never wants trouble"; "He who has a fair wife needs more than two eyes"; "If you marry a beautiful blonde, you marry trouble"; "The wife who loves the looking glass hates the saucepan" (and we all know a lack of domestic skills makes a woman worthless to her husband); "You cannot pluck roses without fear of thorns nor enjoy a fair wife without danger of horns."

"A bad wife ruins a family." That generally occurs when the wife usurps her husband's alleged position as head of the household. Warnings against such a catastrophe start with wedding day superstitions such as "If the newly-married couple were to dance together on their wedding day, the wife would thenceforth rule the roast [roost]." Since most couples dance on their wedding day, maybe it becomes a given then that "He who has a wife has a master" and "A man must ask his wife's leave to thrive." Still, there is shame in such a situation (When a man's a fool, his wife will rule), so husbands are advised "Rule a wife and have a wife."

Meanwhile, wives are given the patronizing consolation that "An obedient wife commands her husband." In reality, "A captain of industry is nothing but a buck private to his wife" and "No man is a hero to his wife or his butler." Sometimes, "A man who is wise is only as wise as his wife thinks he is," and it could be argued that "A true wife is her husband's better half."

The combination of two people in marriage may cause some strange bedfellows: "The calmest husbands make the stormiest wives"; "A deaf husband and a blind wife are always a happy couple" (another slam at a woman's talkative nature and advice to her that it is probably best if she does not see his shenanigans, after all "Discreet wives have sometimes neither eyes nor ears"). Furthermore, "Fat wives make lean husbands" and, conversely, "A light wife makes a heavy husband."

Proverbs that predict a successful couple include: "A warm-back husband and a cold-foot wife should easily lead a compatible life," and "When the husband earns well, the wife spends well," which, according to Thiselton-Dyer, is a variation on the Dutch proverb "When the husband earns well, The wife spins well," meaning the husband and wife love each other and work together.[3]

So, it is possible to find a good wife and that "Saith Solomon the wise" "is a good prize." Furthermore, "A worthy woman is the crown of her husband" and "A good wife and health are man's best wealth." Unfortunately, all three of these proverbs make wives sound like property. Similarly, but with sentiment, there is a proverb that says "A good wife lost is God's gift lost." Still, the proverbs can't resist reminding people that the pendulum could swing either way: "He that has a good wife has an angel by his side; he that has a bad one has a devil at his elbow"; "A man's best fortune, or his worst, is his wife."

If the course of true love does take a bad turn, perhaps it results because "There are men who go to a gymnasium for exercise while their wives are sawing the wood." If a man is self-centered, he will be that irresponsible and will be proud of "the calves of his legs" while his devoted wife is, oddly enough, proud of him. Perhaps he is following the advice of the proverb "Never praise your wife until you have been married ten years." But in that case, "A man who never praises his wife deserves to have a poor one."

That "Husband and wife are one flesh" is a belief reflected in "If the wife sins, the husband is equally guilty." (A Baptist couple explained this relationship to me once, insisting that the husband would be held accountable for his wife on Judgement Day. Since the woman was on her third husband, I wonder how that would work and why women cannot be given so much as the responsibility for their very own souls.) On the other hand, "The wife is the keeper of her husband's conscience as well as his soul."

Fidelity is expected of the wife, but not the husband in proverbs. This double standard is seen in "A faithless wife is the shipwreck of the home" (what about a faithless husband?); "If a man is unfaithful to his wife, it's like spitting from a house into the street; but if a woman is unfaithful to her husband, it's like spitting from the street into the house"; and the use of "man and wife" instead of the parallel "husband and wife."

In summary, one gets the feeling that this entire discussion could be reduced to the opinion that is expressed by one proverb: "A good wife is a perfect lady in the living room, a good cook in the kitchen, and a harlot in the bedroom." In other words, a wife exists to be of service to her husband as a hostess, cook, and lover. Anything else and she is a troublesome shrew who brings a man only misery. To convince men that the risk of getting a bad wife is worth taking, proverbs provide the appropriate propaganda with sayings such as "He that has not got a wife is not yet a complete man"; "A man without a wife is like a fork without a knife"; and "Where there is no wife there is no home." Such sentiment balances out the negative and helps to make the following set of proverbs an intriguing look at the collected wisdom and jaded experience of many centuries.

PROVERBS

General

All are good girls, but where do the bad wives come from? (Spanish; New York)
   Variation: All are good lasses; but where come the ill wives frae? (1866; Scottish)

All married women are not wives.

A bad wife likes to see her husband's heels turned to the door. (Danish; Pacific Northwest)

A bad wife ruins a family. (Chinese)

Better a fortune in a wife than with a wife. (Vermont)

Borrowed wives, like borrowed books, are rarely returned.

But then you know a man can't wive and thrive the same year.

Caesar's wife must be above suspicion.

The calmest husbands make the stormiest wives. (1604; Illinois)

A captain of industry is nothing but a buck private to his wife. (Illinois)

The cunning wife makes her husband her (an) apron. (1866)

A deaf husband and a blind wife are always a happy couple. (1578; German; Illinois, New York, Ohio, Wisconsin)
   Variation: To make a happy couple, the husband must be deaf and the wife blind.

A dirty bread tray tells of a wasteful wife. (North Carolina)

Discreet wives have sometimes neither eyes nor ears. (1594; Shakespeare, *Romeo and Juliet*; Michigan)

A fair wife without a fortune is a fine house without furniture. (1797; English)

A faithless wife is the shipwreck of the home.

Fat wives make lean husbands.

The first wife is matrimony; the second, company; the third, heresy. (1569; Italian)

The first wife remembers everything.

French girls are virtually put on the shelf as soon as the wedding excitement is over.

Generally when a man feels the need of economy he thinks it ought to begin with his wife. (Pacific Northwest)

Give your wife the short knife, keep the long one yourself. (Danish; Pacific Northwest)

God help the man who won't marry until he finds the perfect woman, and God help him still more if he finds her. (Illinois)

God is the guardian of a blind man's wife. (Hindustani)

A good maid sometimes makes a bad wife. (Alabama, Georgia)

A good wife and health are man's best wealth. (1746; Franklin; English; Vermont)

A good wife is a perfect lady in the living room, a good cook in the kitchen, and a harlot in the bedroom. (1942; New York)
   Variation: A wife should be a lady in the parlor, a mother in the kitchen, and a whore in bed.

A good wife is the workmanship of a good husband. (1866)
   Variation: Good wives and good plantations are made by good husbands. (1736; Franklin; New York)
   Variation: A good Jack makes a good Jill.
   [*See also*: A good wife makes a good husband.]

A good wife lost is God's gift lost. (1733; Franklin)

A good wife makes a good husband. (1546; English; Indiana, North Carolina)

Grief for a dead wife, and a troublesome guest, continues to the threshold and there is at rest. But I mean such wives as are none of the best. (1734; Franklin; New York)

A hairy man's rich, a hairy wife's a witch. (North Carolina)

The happiest wife is not she that gets the best husband but she that makes the best of that which she gets. (1913; New York)

He knows little who tells his wife all he knows. (1642; Wisconsin)

He that has a good wife has an angel by his side; he that has a bad one has a devil at his elbow. (Louisiana, Michigan, New York)

He that has not got a wife is not yet a complete man. (1744; Franklin; New York)
   Variation: A man without a wife is but half a man. (1755)

He that hath a fair wife never wants trouble. (Pacific Northwest)
   [*See also*: He who has a fair wife needs more than two eyes.]
   [*See also*: If you marry a beautiful blonde, you marry trouble.]

He that hath a good wife shows it in his dress. (1866)

He that takes a wife takes care. (1495; New York)

He that tells his wife news is but newly married. (1275; German; New Jersey)

He who has a fair wife needs more than two eyes. (1545; New York)
   [*See also*: He that hath a fair wife never wants trouble.]

He who has a wife has a master.
   Variation: He who takes a wife finds a master. (French; Pacific Northwest)

He who hasn't anything to do pulls his wife's eyes out. (New York)

He who loves his wife should watch her. (Arkansas)

He who wishes to chastise a fool, gets him a wife. (1866)

Husband and wife are one flesh. (Yiddish)

If a man is unfaithful to his wife, it's like spitting from a house into the street; but if a woman is unfaithful to her husband, it's like spitting from the street into the house. (North Carolina)

If the newly-married couple were to dance together on their wedding day, the wife would thenceforth rule the roast [*sic*].

If the wife sins, the husband is equally guilty.

If you make your wife an ass, she will make you an ox.

If you marry a beautiful blonde, you marry trouble. (1936; Illinois)
   [See also: He that hath a fair wife never wants trouble.]

If your wife is small, bend down to take her counsel. (1948; New York)

If you take a wife from hell, she will bring you back. (1793)

If you want to know a bad husband, look at his wife's countenance. (Pacific Northwest)

It is a good man that never stumbles, and a good wife that never grumbles.

Variation: "horse" for "man" (Spanish)

It is cheaper to find a wife than to feed a wife. (Illinois)

It's a sweet sorrow to bury a nagging wife.

A kind wife makes a faithful husband. (Michigan)

A light wife makes a heavy husband. (1597; Shakespeare; New York)

Look after your wife; never mind yourself, she'll look after you. (Pacific Northwest)

Lots of men get women, but few get wives. (Kentucky, Tennessee)

A man can't serve two mistresses—his country and his wife.

A man must ask his wife's leave to thrive. (1797; German)
  Variation: A man must ask his wife to thrive. (1866)
  Variation: A man must ask his wife if he may be rich. (Pacific Northwest)
A man's best fortune, or his worst, is his wife. (1795)
  Variation: "virtue" for "fortune" (Spanish)

A man that cheats his wife may cheat many others. (Vermont)

A man who is wise is only as wise as his wife thinks he is. (New York, South Carolina)

A man who kicks his dog will beat his wife. (Kentucky)

The man who never praises his wife deserves to have a poor one. (Pacific Northwest)

A man without a wife is like a fork without a knife. (1866)

Many a man sees a wolf at the door because his wife sees a mink in the window. (Mississippi)

Many blame the wife for their own thriftless life. (1866)

Marriage is the supreme blunder that all women make.

Matrimony is an insane idea on the part of a man to pay some woman's board.
   Variation: Matrimony has been defined to be an insane idea on the part of a man to pay some woman's board. (Texas)

The more men love their glasses, the less they love their wives. (1866)

The most fascinating women never make the best marriages.

Most men get as good a wife as they deserve. (1948; New York)

Motherless husband makes happy wife.
   Variation: She's the happiest wife that marries the son of a dead mother.

A neat maiden often makes a dirty wife.

Ne'er seek a wife till you know what to do with her.

Ne'er take a wife till thou hast a house (and a fire) to put her in. (1733; Franklin)

Never praise your wife until you have been married ten years. (Arkansas)

Next to no wife, a good wife is best. (1497; New Jersey)

A nice wife and a back door oft do make a rich man poor. (1450; English; New York)

A no-account wife takes advice from everyone but her husband. (Mississippi)

No man is a hero to his wife or his butler. (1603)

Nothing on arth puts a feller to his stump like pulling in the same team with a purty gal.

An obedient wife commands her husband. (1866; English)
   Variation: The woman who obeys her husband rules him. (1642; Utah)
   Variation: A virtuous woman commands her husband by obeying him. (Illinois)

An old bachelor is fussy because he has never had a wife to fuss at him. (North Carolina)

One good husband is worth two good wives; for the scarcer things are the more they're valued.

A quiet wife is mighty pretty. (Illinois)

Rather spoil your joke than roil your wife.

Rule a wife and have a wife. (Kentucky, Tennessee)

Saith Solomon the wise, "A good wife is a good prize." (1866)

The second wife always sits on the right knee. (1940; New York)

A sensible wife looks for her enjoyment at "home"—a silly one, "abroad." (Pacific Northwest)

She drove her ducks to a poor market. [She made a bad marriage.] (1939; Indiana)

She that hath a bad husband hath a hell within her own house. (1866)

She that hath an ill husband shows it in her dress. (1866)

She tried it on at first, saying your presence, sir, by going to bed missus and getting up master.

She who marries a man for his money, will have the man but not the money. (Washington)

The shoemaker's wife goes barefoot.
    Variation: Shoemakers' wives are the worst shod.
    Variation: The smith's mare and the cobbler's wife are always the worst shod.

Take a friend for what he does, a wife for what she has, and goods for what they are worth. (Illinois, Ohio)

There are men who go to a gymnasium for exercise while their wives are sawing the wood. (Pacific Northwest)

There is many a good wife that can't sing and dance well. (1866)

There is one good wife in the country, and every man thinks he hath her. (1866)

They all know what to do with a bad wife but he who's got one. (1621; Utah)

A true wife is her husband's better half. (Mississippi)
  Variation: A true wife is her husband's flower of beauty. (Mississippi)
  Variation: A true wife is her husband's heart's treasure. (Mississippi)

A true wife is proud of her husband; he, the calves of his legs. (Pacific Northwest)

Two good days for a man in his life: when he weds, and when he buries his wife.

Want makes strife between man and wife. (1732; Illinois)

A warm-back husband and a cold-foot wife should easily lead a compatible life. (Vermont)

When a man's a fool, his wife will rule.

When a man takes a wife, he ceases to dread hell. (California)

When the good man is from home, the good wife's table is soon spread.

When the husband earns well, the wife spends well. (Wisconsin)

When the husband's away, the wife will play. (Tennessee)

When you choose a wife shut your eyes and commend your soul to God. (Spanish; Pacific Northwest)

Where there is no wife there is no home.

Who finds a wife finds a good thing. (1948; New York)

Who has a bad wife, has purgatory for a neighbor. (1866)

Who is the wife of one cannot eat the rice of two. (Indiana)

A wife can make or break her husband. [financially] (Yiddish)

Wife, from thy spouse each blemish hide, more than from the world beside.

A wife is a young man's slave and an old man's darling. (1546; English; Illinois)
   Variation: Better be an old man's darling, than a young man's slave. [warling] (Vermont)
   Variation: It is better to be an old man's darling, than a poor man's slave. (Nebraska)

A wife is seen with pleasure only at the wedding and in the winding sheet. (1786)

The wife is the keeper of her husband's conscience as well as his soul.

Wife, make thine own candle, Spare penny to handle. [thrifty] (1940; New York)

The wife who loves the looking-glass hates the saucepan.

A worthy woman is the crown of her husband. (1948; New York)

You cannot pluck roses without fear of thorns nor enjoy a fair wife without danger of horns. (Wisconsin)

A young woman married to an old man must behave like an old woman.

Brides

Being a wife starts with being a bride. Because this occasion is so enormously special, brides gets separate attention from the proverbs as noted below. There is no great mystery to any of these proverbs, although two deal with superstitions (Always a bridesmaid, but never a bride; A sad bride makes a glad wife). "Happy the bride the sun shines on" "had once a practical application when marriages were celebrated in the church porch. A wet day on such an occasion was a serious matter."[4] Otherwise, the remaining proverbs are, like most proverbs, expressions of observations of life.

Afoot and alone, as the gal went to be married.

All brides are child brides in their mother's eyes. (New York)

Always a bridesmaid, but never a bride. (Pennsylvania)
   Variation: "often" for "always" and no "but"
   Variation: Always a maiden, never a wife.
   Variation: Three times a bridesmaid, but never a bride. [other similar constructions]

As flat as a bride's biscuits.

At a wedding feast, the one to eat the least is the bride. (Spanish)

Bridesmaids may soon be made brides.

Happy the bride the sun shines on. (1648)
   Variation: Happy the bride the sun shines on and happy the corpse the rain pours on.

It's a poor bride who cannot help some. (Vermont)

A rich bride goes young to the church. (Wisconsin)

A sad bride makes a glad wife. (Illinois)

The same flowers that adorn a bride are placed on a corpse.

Shinin' like a gal's face when she's a fixin' to be married.

NOTES

1. Thomas Firminger Thiselton-Dyer, *Folklore of Women* (Chicago: A. C. McClurg, 1906), 170.
   2. Ibid., 162.
   3. Ibid., 160.
   4. Ibid., 208–9.

2

A WOMAN'S NATURE

Remarks about the behavior of women and relationships with them, that is, what is in their nature and what one can expect from them, are very common among American proverbs about women. There is a diversity of comments ranging from tribute to tirade (Nature meant woman to be her masterpiece; Women are the root of all evil), yet the negative and sarcastic dominate.

Women, it appears, aren't worth much (A man of straw is worth a woman of gold; All women are good; good for something or good for nothing) unless they are prime goods on the market (A simple maiden in her flower is worth a hundred coats-of-arms [referring to virginity]). A man had better hurry, though, before the prize is spoiled since "Maids are drawn to pleasure as moths to the flame." Even then, the prize may not be worth the price because "Maids want nothing but husbands, and then they want everything."

Similarly, "Grasp at a woman and hold a nettle." Such a warning is repeatedly given by the proverbs about the trouble women cause (The fewer the women, the less the trouble; There is no mischief but a woman is at the heart of it; Where there's a woman, there's trouble; A woman is at the bottom of every lawsuit). Women are probably so much trouble because they are conniving by nature (Female is one head with two faces; A woman knows a bit more than Satan). Consequently, "Woman is woe to man" because "Any girl can handle the beast in a man if she's cagey enough" and "play the deuce with a fellow." That is why "The female of the species is more deadly than the male."

Furthermore, "The female's cunning is equal to her obstinacy": "No argument can convince a woman or a stubborn ass"; "An opinion formed by a woman is inflexible; the fact is not half so stubborn"; "A woman convinced against her will, Is of the same opinion still." Because of her stubbornness, "Never quarrel with a woman" for "A woman must have her way" (Thou lovest thine own will; but as for that matter show me the woman that does not), and that can be a "dangerous ill" considering that a woman's proverbial reputation includes "Hell hath no fury like a woman scorned"; "No fish without bone; no woman without a temper"; "A woman's vengeance knows no bounds"; and "You get a woman mad and her blood good and hot, better let her blood cool for she'll sho' hurt you."

"Women are strong when they arm themselves with their weaknesses," and one of those is tears. There are nine proverbs in this collection whose subject is tears, thus attesting to the extent of the belief that a woman's tears may not be sincere, but a man is honor-bound to assuage them: "Every woman is wrong until she cries, and then she is right instantly"; "Men aren't worth the salt of a woman's tears"; "Men should be careful lest they cause women to weep, for God counts their tears"; "Nothing dries sooner that a woman's tears"; "Weeping like a girl"; "A woman's strongest weapons are her tears"; "A woman's tears are a fountain of craft"; "Women have tears at command"; "Women laugh when they can and weep when they will."

Tears are just part of what contributes to women being considered the weaker sex. (Frailty, your name is woman.) Proverbs describe the woman as "pale and spoony" with a heart as soft as cushions. The ideal for a woman is to be a delicate lady who "takes a pin to eat a pea" and who would find it "hard to be a biddy and a lady too." The proverbs seem to have quite an interest in the woman's role as a lady: "It's a poor house that can't support one lady"; "A lady is known by the product she endorses"; "Once a lady, always a lady"; "You mustn't rush a lady."

It is contradictory to talk about women being conniving and getting their way and then describe them as weak and soft. The explanation of this contradiction might be that men want women to be weak so they can be dominated, thus they complain when women show any strength. It is also contradictory to glorify the status of being a lady, then say "All women and cats are black in darkness," "All women look the same after the sun goes down," and "The Colonel's lady and Judy O'Grady are sisters under the skin." These latter proverbs indicate an attitude that all women have the same value no matter what their clothes or manners or virtue because their only real purpose is for sex.

If there appears to be confusion expressed as to the merit of women, perhaps it is because the male authors of the proverbs felt that "Woman brings to man the greatest blessing and the greatest plague." If a woman is a mystery to a man, perhaps it is because "Woman is the key to life's mystery." In short, to men "A woman is the greatest contradiction of all."

It's the nature of things for women to behave in certain ways, the proverbs seem to say, and it's unnatural for women to behave in certain other ways (a point emphasized in chapter 8, "A Woman's Place"). Despite the proverb, "There are two kinds of women: those who take what you are and those who take what you have," proverbs provide a long list of other characteristics for women: They are slow, gentle, bashful, never satisfied, vivacious, affectionate, and curious. Women are the devil's nets and queer cattle. Women have fears but no souls. "Music is the key to the female heart." "A woman is known by her walking and drinking." "Women are wise on a sudden, fools on premeditation."

The proverbs have an unkindly way of saying that a woman wants attention (She wants to be the bride at every wedding and the corpse at every funeral; A woman that loves to be at the windows is like a bunch of grapes in the highway) and she wants romance (Once a woman gives you her heart you can never get rid of the rest of her; A woman's whole life is a history of the affections).

One could not discuss the nature of women without touching upon the subject of intelligence, which is an eternal topic in the battle of the sexes. Because it has long been thought that "Little girls have little wit" and that "It takes as much wit not to displease a woman as it takes little to please her," women have had to play dumb to play it safe: "It takes a smart woman to be a fool." So, "A man thinks he knows, but a woman knows better." Besides, "Stupidity in a woman is unfeminine" so "A woman conceals what she knows not."

There are proverbs that discuss the characteristics of men, too, and sometimes the two go together: "Thrift is to a man what chastity is to a woman"; " A gracious woman retains honor (and strong men retain their riches)"; and "Man gets and forgets, woman gives and forgives." The first two proverbs mean that men are concerned with the value of money while women are concerned with the value of their reputations, once again indicating that to men brute force and money are power while a woman's only power rests in charm and sexual favors. (Beware, though: "Woman learns how to hate when she has lost the ability to charm.") The latter proverb means that men are self-centered takers who use other people for their own ends while women are the nurturers and peacemakers.

There are too many proverbs in this category to mention them all. Suffice it to say that "Girls will be girls"—whatever that is—and "a woman is always a woman." To men, "Woman—she shares our griefs, doubles our joys and trebles our expenses" probably sums up their opinion of women. Yet they also admit "Everything goes to loose ends where there is no woman." Wanting to feel needed, too, men say "A woman without a man is like a handle without a pan." To women, reality is

"What ever women do they must do twice as well as men to be thought half as good. Luckily, this is not difficult."

PROVERBS

General

All women and cats are black in darkness. (1745; Wisconsin)

All women are good; good for something or good for nothing. (1866; English)

All women look the same after the sun goes down. (1948; Illinois)

The American woman, if left to her own devices, washes on Monday, irons on Tuesday, bakes on Wednesday, and marries on Thursday.

Any girl can handle the beast in a man if she's cagey enough. (Mississippi)

As great a pity to see a woman weep as to see a goose go barefoot. [They do it all the time, so no cause for concern.] (1523)

But now he is as pale and spoony as a milliner's girl.

The Colonel's lady and Judy O'Grady are sisters under the skin.
    Variation: Judy O'Grady and the Colonel's lady. . . . (North Carolina)

Confound this powder—it's as slow as a woman.

Cushions as soft as a young gal's heart.

A dainty lady takes a pin to eat a pea. (Jamaica, North Carolina)

Everything goes to loose ends where there is no woman.

Every woman is wrong until she cries, and then she is right instantly.

Every woman keeps a corner in her heart where she is always twenty-one. (Illinois, New York)

Female is one head with two faces. (Florida)

The female of the species is more deadly than the male. (from *The Female of the Species* by Rudyard Kipling [1865–1935])
  Variation: The female is the more deadly of the species. (1911)

The female's cunning is equal to her obstinacy.

The fewer the women, the less the trouble. (Illinois)

Frailty, your name is woman. (1600; Shakespeare; German; Minnesota, New York)

Girls will be girls. (American)

A gracious woman retains honor. (And strong men retain their riches)

Grasp at a woman and hold a nettle. (1817)

He gets on best with women who know best how to get along without them.

He is as gentle as a woman when he has no rival near him.

Hell hath no fury like a woman scorned. (1625; Illinois, New Jersey, Oregon)
  Variation: Hell knows no wrath like a woman scorned.

He was as bashful as a girl.

How many times, while sighing, is a woman laughing. (Mexican-American)

Is a woman ever satisfied? No, if she were she wouldn't be a woman. (New Jersey)

It is hard to be a biddy and a lady too.
  [It is hard to be the maid and the hostess at the same time.] (New York, South Carolina)

It's a poor house that can't afford one lady.
  Variation: "support" for "afford" (Kansas, New York)

It takes a smart woman to be a fool. (Maryland)

It takes as much wit not to displease a woman as it takes little to please her. (Pacific Northwest)

A lady is known by the product she endorses. (1936; New York, South Carolina)

Little girls have little wit. (American)

Long thread, lazy girl. (Washington)

Maids are drawn to pleasure as moths to the flame.

Maids want nothing but husbands, and then they want everything. (1678; English)

Man gets and forgets, woman gives and forgives. (New York, South Carolina)

A man of straw is worth a woman of gold. (1866; French)

A man thinks he knows, but a woman knows better. (1938)

Men aren't worth the salt of a woman's tears. (Vermont)

Men should be careful lest they cause women to weep, for God counts their tears. (Pacific Northwest)

The mistress makes the morning, But the Lord makes the afternoon.

Music is the key to the female heart. (Illinois)

Nature meant woman to be her masterpiece.

Never quarrel with a woman. (1875; Chinese; Indiana)

No argument can convince a woman or a stubborn ass.
    Variation: "will" for "can" (Illinois, North Carolina)

No fish without bone; no woman without a temper.

Nothing dries sooner than a woman's tears. (1563; Oklahoma, Texas)

Oh a woman is always a woman.

Once a lady, always a lady. (New York, South Carolina)

Once a woman gives you her heart you can never get rid of the rest of her. (1696; Illinois)

One girl is a girl, two girls are half a girl, and three girls are no girl at all. (1930; Kentucky, Tennessee)

The only way to get the upper hand of a woman is not to be more woman than she is herself. (Pacific Northwest)

An opinion formed by a woman is inflexible; the fact is not half so stubborn. (Pacific Northwest)

Our girlhood determines our womanhood. (Florida)

The premonitory symptoms of love are as evident to a woman as are those of any other eruptive disease about to break out to a Philadelphia doctor.

She's one of the old blue hen's chickens. [i.e., a hellcat, a termagant] (Texas)

She wants to be the bride at every wedding and the corpse at every funeral. (Washington)

A simple maiden in her flower is worth a hundred coats-of-arms. [virginity]

A small sprinkling of the feminine gender, jest enough to take the cuss off, and no more.

Smelt as sweet as a gal's breath.

Stupidity in a woman is unfeminine.

There are two kinds of women: those who take what you are and those who take what you have. (New Jersey, North Carolina)

There is no mischief but a woman is at the heart of it.
    Variation: There is no mischief done, but a woman is one.
    Variation: There is no mischief in the world done, but a woman is always one. (1866)
    [*See also*: There's hardly a strife . . . under Law]

Thou lovest thine own will; but as for that matter show me the woman that does not. (Pacific Northwest)

Thrift is to a man what chastity is to a woman. (1937; New York, South Carolina)

Too much whiskey will kill; too many women will chill.

Vivacity is the gift of woman. (Illinois)

Weeping like a girl.

What ever women do they must do twice as well as men to be thought half as good. Luckily, this is not difficult.

Where there's a woman, there's trouble.

Woman brings to man the greatest blessing and the greatest plague. (1948; Illinois)

A woman can play the deuce (devil) with a fellow.

A woman conceals what she knows not. (1386; Chaucer; Oklahoma, Texas)
   Variation: A woman conceals what she does not know. (French; Pacific Northwest)

A woman convinced against her will, Is of the same opinion still. (North Carolina)
   Variation: "lady persuaded" for "woman convinced") (Kansas, Ohio)

A woman is at the bottom of every lawsuit.
   Variation: There is scarcely a lawsuit unless a woman is the cause of it.

A woman is known by her walking and drinking. (Spanish; New York)

A woman is the greatest contradiction of all. (Illinois)
   Variation: Woman at best is a contradiction still. [from Pope's "Moral Essays"] (Pacific Northwest)

Woman is the key to life's mystery.

Woman is woe to man. (1700)

A woman knows a bit more than Satan. (1559; Illinois)

Woman learns how to hate when she has lost the ability to charm.

A woman listens to a play with her mind and judges it with her senses. (Pacific Northwest)

Woman must have her way. (1774)
  Variation: A woman will always have her way.
  Variation: Woman will have both her word and her way. (Illinois, New York)
  Variation: Man has his will, but woman has her way.
  Variation: A woman has her way.

A woman's friendship is, as a rule, the legacy of love or the alms of indifference. (Pacific Northwest)

Woman—she shares our griefs, doubles our joys and trebles our expenses. (Pacific Northwest)

A woman spins even while she talks.

A woman's strongest weapons are her tears. (Pacific Northwest)

A woman's tears are a fountain of craft. (English; Pacific Northwest)

A woman's vengeance knows no bounds. (German)

A woman's whole life is a history of the affections. (New York)

A woman that loves to be at the windows is like a bunch of grapes in the highway. (1804)

Woman thy name is curiosity. (1775)

The woman who likes washing can always find water.

A woman without a man is like a handle without a pan. (1867)

A woman without religion is a flower without perfume. A man without religion is a horse without a bridle.

Women and dogs set men together by the ears. (1639; Illinois, New York)

Women and elephants never forget. (1910; Illinois)

Women and their wills are dangerous ills.

Women are a good deal like licker, ef you love 'em too hard thar sure to throw you some way.

Women are always in extremes. (1526; Illinois, New York)
   Variation: Women are in extremes, they are better or worse than men. (French)

Women are kittle (queer) cattle.

Women are saints in church, angels in the street, devils in the kitchen, apes in bed. (1559; Illinois)

Women are strong when they arm themselves with their weaknesses.

Women are the devil's nets. (1520; Illinois)

Women are the root of all evil. (1948; Wisconsin)

Women are wise on a sudden, fools on premeditation. (1866)
   Variation: Women are wise impromptu, fools on reflection. (Italian)

Women be forgetful, Children be unkind, Executors are covetous and take what they can find.

Women can tolerate everything—except each other.

Women commend an honest man: but they do not like him.
   Variation: Women commend a modest man but like him not.

Women confess their small faults that their candor may cover great ones.

Women do not read; they listen with the eye. (Pacific Northwest)

Women forgive injuries but never forget slights. (1843; New York)

Women have no souls. (1638)

Women have tears at command. (1712)

Women have their fears.

Women laugh when they can and weep when they will. (1866; French)
   Variation: . . . and cry when they want to. (Mexican-American)
   Variation: A woman laughs when she can and weeps when she pleases.
   Variation: A woman laughs when she can but cries whenever she wishes. (1570; New Jersey)

Women, like princes, find few *real* friends. (Pacific Northwest)

Women must always have the last word.
   Variation: Women will have the last word (1541; Illinois, New York)
   Variation: A woman has the last word.

Women rouge that they may not blush. (Italian)

Women sometimes exaggerate a little, and this is an important point to be remembered by men and women. (Wisconsin)

You can never tell about women, but if you can, you shouldn't.

You can take the girl out of the country, but you can't take the country out of the girl. (Illinois, Kansas)
   Variation: You can take a girl off a farm, but you can't take the farm out of a girl.

You can't live with them (women/men) and you can't live without them. (Washington)

You get a woman mad and her blood good and hot, better let her blood cool for she'll sho' hurt you. (South Carolina)

You mustn't rush a lady. (Ohio)

3

A WOMAN'S LOOKS

Ugly, homely, painted or plain, pretty in figure or dress—did it matter more to the beauty or her beholder? It is hard to tell from the proverbs on the subject. What is obvious, though, is the sizable attention paid by proverbs to a woman's looks, female vanity, and the rewards or impediments that seem to accompany appearance.

Part of the feminist debate has been an outcry against the exaggerated importance placed on a woman's appearance. The attitude has been that a woman's only value rested in her beauty. An obvious example is the fact that there are beauty pageants for women but not for men. Even worse, for many women, beauty pageants are their only means of getting scholarships and career advancements; that is to say that there are not enough avenues open to women that allow them to succeed based on their brains, so women have to resort to other ways of opening doors. "A man without ambition is like a woman without looks" tells us that a man can succeed with just honest effort, but a woman's efforts are for nought unless she is good-looking, too. This proverb also explains why it is acceptable, even expected, for a man to be aggressive at his job, but a woman is considered unfeminine and bossy if she is ambitious.

Although some proverbs admit that there are values in a woman that can be more important than beauty, the emphasis is still on pleasing men (Good looks in a woman haint wuth as much to a man as good cookin' and savin' ways). In fact, having a beauty around might be a dangerous temptation according to Benjamin Franklin (who was an authority on falling to temptation): "Let thy maid servant be faithful, strong and homely."

In a twisted way, ugliness can even be seen as a benefit because at least then a woman is safe from being attacked by lascivious men (Plain women are as safe as churches; Ugliness is the guardian of women). In fact, "A woman and a cherry are painted for their own harm" is a reference to the once-held belief that rouging was a sign of a fast woman. It doesn't occur to men that women might want to be spruced-up for their own sense of self-worth (The blind man's wife needs no makeup). So, plainness and modesty were regarded as companion attributes. Nonetheless, "She who is born beautiful is born married" even if "The ugliest girl makes the best housewife."

Such contradiction abounds in proverbs when it comes to beauty in women. While women are prized for their looks, they are, at the same time, criticized for their efforts to enhance those looks with constant complaints about the time and expense invested in clothes, makeup, and hairstyles (She was melted and poured into her dress; She's painted up like a wild Indian; The smiles of the pretty woman are the tears of the purse). Men probably object to the expense because of their own greed: "Beauties without fortune have sweethearts plenty but husbands none at all" tells us that in the final analysis men are more attracted to money. But women have a problem with money, too: "A poor beauty is in double jeopardy: her beauty tempts others, her poverty herself."

Even though "You can't know a girl by her looks" and "There's not a pretty girl without fault, nor an ugly one without charm," those who aren't outwardly beautiful aren't given much of a chance to demonstrate other values because ugliness is ostracized and ridiculed (Don't dare kiss an ugly girl—she'll tell the world about it; Compliment an old hag on her lovely appearance and she'll take you at your word). However, it is tit for tat: "An ugly man never gets a pretty wife."

Then there is the ever-popular running joke about a woman and her age (For example: The longest five years in a woman's life is between twenty-nine and thirty; A woman over thirty who will tell her exact age will tell anything.) This obsession with age is just another way of saying that a woman's worth is dependent on how she looks: Old and wrinkled is not desirable, as evidenced by the number of older men who abandon their wives for younger women, yet the reverse seldom happens.

So, the men seem to put a premium on a woman's beauty, but, naturally, they claim it is the women who have a problem and that problem is vanity. "Vanity thy name is woman," is probably the most well-known proverb of several on the subject. Beauty and vanity have been so intermingled in common perception that until recent times women were required by many denominations to wear a hat or other head-covering to church because "A woman's hair is her crowning glory," and she should be too modest to show it off in church where God's glory should shine most prominently.

Actually, the problem is the pressure put on women to be pretty, so when women are told that "No woman is ugly if she is well-dressed" should it be a surprise that "A woman doesn't worry as much over how she is to gain a crown of glory as she does how to gain a new bonnet"? Or that "A woman's bonnet must be orthodox before her prayer-book is"? Of course, it is not a compliment to say that women would "rather be pretty than have a good brain," but how else are women to react when the dominant males indicate that looks are more important than intelligence? Men may say that "too much gilding makes men suspicious" yet women know that "Women's jars breed men's wars," that is, feminine beauty can cause a man to go to great lengths for her. So, is it that "You may know a foolish woman by her finery" or a clever woman who knows how to survive in a man's world?

Modern society is struggling with further complications of this emphasis on looks with the rise of bulimia and anorexia, eating disorders that are almost exclusively a female problem and that arise from the woman's mania for being thin and pretty. The prevalence of these disorders, the continued existence of beauty pageants, the use of scantily clad women as "entertainment," the paucity of substantive roles for women in the movies because of a prevalent portrayal of women as sex objects only, the gender bias in the classroom—all indicate that women still have a long way to go in proving their value to society as complete human beings capable of making worthwhile contributions in every field.

PROVERBS

General

All painted and varnished up as neat and shining as one of your New York gal's faces on a Sunday.

Beauties without fortunes have sweethearts plenty, but husbands none at all. (1866)

The best-dressed woman usually arrives with the least. [selfish]
   Variation: The best-dressed woman usually arrives last with the least.

Big woman, small feet; Small woman, all feet. (Washington)

The blind man's wife needs no makeup.
   Variation: Why does the blind man's wife paint herself? (1736; Franklin)

Variation: The blind man's wife needs no painting. (1659; German, Spanish; 1736, Franklin; New York, South Carolina)

Compliment an old hag on her lovely appearance and she'll take you at your word.

Don't dare kiss an ugly girl—she'll tell the world about it.

A fire scorches from near, a beautiful woman from near and from far. (Wisconsin)

The first girl up in the morning is the best-dressed girl that day. [an appeal to vanity to encourage industriousness] (Illinois)

Food and woman must go in [be appreciated] through the eyes. (1962; Mexican-American)

The good-looking woman needs no paint. (Illinois)

Good looks in a woman haint wuth as much to a man as good cookin' and savin' ways. (North Carolina)

Ladies young and fair have the gift to know it. (1599; Shakespeare; Kansas, New York, South Carolina)

Let thy maid servant be faithful, strong and homely. (1736; Franklin)

A little bit of powder and a little bit of paint makes a woman look like what she ain't.
    Variation: . . . makes an ugly woman . . .
    Variation: . . . makes you . . .
    Variation: Powder and paint make a girl look what she ain't.

The longest five years in a woman's life is between twenty-nine and thirty.

A man without ambition is like a woman without looks. (1900; New York)

The most dreadful thing against women is the character of the men that praise them. (Pacific Northwest)

No woman is ugly if she is well-dressed. (Spanish, Portuguese)
   Variation: No woman is ugly when she is dressed. (1866)

No woman should ever be quite accurate about her age: it looks so calculating. (New York)

The old cat refuses to admit that the face in the looking glass is her own.

Plain women are as safe as churches. (Illinois)

A poor beauty is in double jeopardy: her beauty tempts others, her poverty herself.

Shame in a woman is known by her dress. (1963; Mexican-American)

She has on a brand splinterfire new dress. (Texas)

She's painted up like a wild Indian. (Texas)

She was melted and poured into her dress. (North Carolina)

She who dresses in black must rely on her beauty. (Mexican-American)
   [*See also*: The woman who dresses in yellow trusts her beauty.]

She who is born beautiful is born married. (English)
   Variation: "handsome" for "beautiful" (1866)
   Variation: She that is born a beauty, is born half-married. (1798)
   Variation: She who is a beauty is half married; She who is born beautiful is half married. (1732; Illinois, New York, Vermont)

The smiles of the pretty woman are the tears of the purse.
   Variation: When a handsome woman laughs you may be sure her purse weeps. (Italian)

Tell a woman she's a beauty and the devil will tell her it ten times. (1732; Italian, Spanish; Illinois)
   Variation: Once tell a woman she's a beauty and the devil will tell her so ten times.

That woman is young that does not look a day older than she says she is. (Mississippi)
   [*See also*: A woman is as old as she looks.]

There never was a mirror that told a woman she was ugly. (French)
  Variation: Never a looking glass told a woman she was ugly. (Pacific Northwest)

There's not a pretty girl without fault, nor an ugly one without charm. (1963; Mexican-American)

The ugliest girl makes the best housewife.

The ugliest woman can look in the mirror and think she is beautiful. (1948; North Carolina)

Ugliness is the guardian of women. (Hebrew; Illinois)

An ugly baby makes a pretty girl. (North Carolina)

An ugly man never gets a pretty wife. (North Carolina)

An ugly woman dreads the mirror. (Japanese; Illinois)

Vanity acts like a woman—they both think they lose something when love or praise is accorded to another. (Pacific Northwest)

Vanity, thy name is woman. (Pacific Northwest)

A woman and a cherry are painted for their own harm. (1659; Spanish; Michigan)

A woman doesn't worry as much over how she is to gain a crown of glory as she does how she is to gain a new bonnet. (Pacific Northwest)

A woman is as old as she admits.

A woman is as old as she looks. A man is old when he quits looking. (South Carolina)
  Variation: A woman is no older than she looks. (And a man than he feels.) (Alabama, Georgia, Texas)
  Variation: A man is as old as he feels, and a woman as old as she looks. (California, Vermont)
  [*See also*: That woman is young that does not look a day older than she says she is.]

A woman need not always recall her age, but she should never forget it. (Pacific Northwest)

A woman over thirty who will tell her exact age will tell anything. (New York)

A woman's bonnet must be orthodox before her prayer-book is. (Pacific Northwest)

A woman's hair is her crowning glory. (1948; New York)

The woman who dresses in silk stays at home. [too delicate to venture out] (1963; Mexican-American)

The woman who dresses in yellow trusts her beauty. (1963; Mexican-American)
   [*See also*: She who dresses in black must rely on her beauty.]

A woman who looks much in the glass spins but little. (1623; Wisconsin)

Women are ambulating blocks for millinery. (Mississippi)

Women are like books; too much gilding makes men suspicious that the binding is the most important part.

Women are wacky, women are vain; they'd rather be pretty than have a good brain. (1940; New York)

Women's jars breed men's wars. (English; Pacific Northwest)

Women swallow at one mouthful the lie that flatters and drink drop by drop the truth that is bitter. (Pacific Northwest)

You can't know a girl by her looks or a man by his books.

You may know a foolish woman by her finery. (1866)

4

MOTHERS AND DAUGHTERS

More phone calls are made on Mother's Day than on any other occasion during the year. This devotion to one's mother naturally carries over into proverbs where mother is a doting saint (God could not be everywhere, therefore He made mothers; Heaven is at the feet of mothers; There is no such thing as a bad mother) who is so convinced that her child is perfect or handsome that "If you take the child by the hand, you take the mother by the heart."

But, if a mother is so "blind she can't tell black from white" concerning her children, then someone might warn her that "Mother's darlings make but milk-porridge heroes." According to Thiselton-Dyer, this proverb was used to correct women lest they become too lenient.[1] "Better the child's cry" now in punishment "than the mother's sigh" later after a monster has been created.

Even then, though, "A mother's love will dash up from the depths of the sea" because a "Mother's love is best of all." A mother is tender, knows best, and is so attentive to her child that you'd have to be in dreadful shape before "Your own mother wouldn't know you."* The worst offense to someone is to insult that person's mother (Your mother wears combat boots—another sexist expression that implies that a woman serving her country is an unfeminine aberration).

Stepmothers and mothers-in-law are a totally different story: "There are as many good step-mothers as white ravens"; "There is only one good

---

*Despite this bond, ungrateful children might neglect their mother in her time of need (A mother can take care of ten children, but sometimes ten children can't take care of one mother).

mother-in-law and she is dead." Mothers-in-law are particularly vilified in proverbs, perhaps because "The mother-in-law is a queer invention, as full of flaws and dangers as a second-hand boiler." We are told that a mother-in-law is prone to getting drunk and vengeful (When the cask is full the mother-in-law gets drunk; When mothers-in-law fall out, then we get at the family facts). Apparently, the problem is that "The mother-in-law remembers not that she was a daughter-in-law" and complains that "A bad daughter-in-law is worse than a thousand devils." So, she makes life miserable for the daughter-in-law (Always sweep where your mother-in-law looks) who probably also doesn't realize that "Daughters-in-law become mothers-in-law."

Nearly every proverb about both mothers and daughters is a dictum that says daughters will grow up to be just like their mothers (Like mother, like daughter; Observe the mother and take the daughter) or just the opposite (Light-heel'd mothers make leaden-heeled daughters). The fear in raising a daughter is that she won't learn her trade, that of being a wife (A diamond daughter turns to glass as a wife [probably too spoiled]; An undutiful daughter will prove an unmanageable wife) or that she will not be marriageable in the first place (It is harder to marry a daughter well than to bring her up well). Consequently, it was important to "see her in company" "for then she will cultivate every charm to make herself as attractive as possible."[2] In other words, parents should push a daughter out into society because if she hides at home she will sour and never get a proposal.

Daughters were seen as a financial burden because they would be trained for frying up the bacon instead of bringing it home, so the predominant concern has been marrying them off (Marry your son when you will, your daughter when you can; Marry your daughter and eat fresh fish betimes [which means that the marriage of one's daughter, like the eating of fresh fish, should be done as soon as possible.[3]]). Thus, the raising of a daughter is actually the process of making a good daughter-in-law, that is, a marketable commodity (You speak to the daughter, and mean the daughter-in law; A good daughter makes a good daughter-in-law).

Part of the necessity for unloading daughters resulted from the practice of a woman taking her husband's name upon marriage, which prevents her from carrying on her own family's name. Therefore, a daughter was extra baggage and not truly part of the family lineage. Her value came in "giving the bride away" and making successful alliances thereby.

A daughter is "brittle ware" who must always be protected from evil predators (See how the boy is with his sister and you can know how the man will be with your daughter). She is always a responsibility as shown by the practice of the bride being taken down the aisle by one man, her father, and handed over to the care of another man, her husband (My son is my son till he gets him a wife; but my daughter's my daughter all the days of her life). The modern woman has an independence that challenges these proverbs, yet most still marry in ceremonies that follow these customs and most still subjugate themselves to their husband's superior identity by using his name. Maybe "No Indian ever sold his daughter for a name," but many families, many women themselves, still do.

The following proverbs are presented in five groups: mothers, mothers-in-law, mothers and daughters, daughters, and daughters-in-law.

PROVERBS

Mothers

Better the child's cry than the mother's sigh.

Every child is perfect to its mother. (English; North Carolina)

Every mother's child is handsome.
Variation: Every mother thinks her child is beautiful. (Yiddish)
Variation: No mother has a homely child. (Wisconsin)
Variation: There's only one pretty child in the world, and every mother has it. (German)
Variation: A mother almost always thinks her young one handsomer than any body else's.)

A father to his desk, a mother to her dishes. (Illinois)

God could not be everywhere; therefore, He made mothers.

Heaven is at the feet of mothers. (Illinois)

If you don't obey your mother, you will obey your stepmother. [Don't worry your mother to death] (Wisconsin)

If you take the child by the hand, you take the mother by the heart.

I'm as tender as a mother to you.

It's a wise child that knows his own mother in a bathing suit. [extremes of fashion] (English; North Carolina,

It takes a mother to be so blind she can't tell black from white. (Colorado)

John Do-little was the son of good-wife Spin-little. (1808)

June brides, January mothers. (New York)

A mother can take care of ten children, but sometimes ten children can't take care of one mother. (Jewish)

Mother knows best. (1958)
   Variation: Mother knows best; father pays less. (1927)

The mother knows best whether the child is like the father.

Mother's darlings make but milk-porridge heroes. (1798)

Mother's love is best of all. (1814; Wisconsin)

A mother's love will dash up from the depths of the sea.

A mother's tears are the same in all languages. (Pacific Northwest)

Step on a crack, break your mother's back. [bad luck]

There are as many good step-mothers as white ravens. (1640; Illinois)

There is no such thing as a bad mother. (Yiddish)

Your mother wears combat boots. (North Carolina)

Your own mother wouldn't know you.

Mothers-in-Law

Always sweep where your mother-in-law looks. (New Mexico)

Mother-in-law and daughter-in-law are a tempest in a hailstorm.

The mother-in-law is a queer invention, as full of flaws and dangers as a second-hand boiler.

The mother-in-law remembers not that she was a daughter-in-law. (1594; Minnesota, North Carolina)
   Variation: No mother-in-law ever remembers that she was once a daughter-in-law.

There is only one good mother-in-law, and she is dead.

When mothers-in-law fall out, then we get at the family facts. (Spanish; Pacific Northwest)

When the cask is full the mother-in-law gets drunk.

Mothers and Daughters

The daughter of a good mother will be the mother of a good daughter.

The daughter of a spry old woman makes a poor housekeeper. (Mississippi)

Everyone can keep house better than her mother, till she trieth. (1795)

He who would the daughter win, with the mother must begin. (1578)
   Variation: He that would the daughter win would with the mother begin.
   Variation: Sweet-talk the old lady to get the daughter.
   Variation: Who the daughter would win with mama must begin.
   Variation: Salt the cow and catch the calf. (Welsh)

Light-heel'd mothers make leaden-heeled daughters. (1745; Franklin)

Like mother, like daughter. (1300; American, 1644; English; North Carolina)
   Variation: As is the mother, so is the daughter. (1300)

A mother wants her daughter married well, but her sister doesn't want her married better than she is. (California)

Observe the mother and take the daughter. (Wisconsin)

The old woman would not have sought her daughter in the oven if she had not been there herself.

Daughters

Daughters are brittle ware. (Illinois)

Deacons' daughters and ministers' sons are the biggest devils that ever run. (1855; Vermont)

A diamond daughter turns to glass as a wife. (New Jersey)

Every girl is beautiful in her father's eyes. (Illinois)

First a daughter, then a son, and the family's well begun. (New York)

It is harder to marry a daughter well than to bring her up well. (1732; North Dakota)

The man had three or four daughters who, as the phrase goes, "gave you a good deal for your money." [i.e., were entertaining]

Marry your daughter and eat fresh fish betimes. (1736; Franklin)

Marry your son when you will, your daughter when you can. (1734; Franklin; New York, Vermont)
   Variation: Marry your son when you please, and your daughter when you can. (1640; Indiana, New York)

My son is my son till he gets him a wife; but my daughter's my daughter all the days of her life. (1670; English)
   Variation: A daughter is a daughter all the days of her life, but a son is a son till he gets him a wife.

No Indian ever sold his daughter for a name. (Oklahoma)

See how the boy is with his sister and you can know how the man will be with your daughter. (Plains Sioux)

See your sons and daughters: they are your future. (Oneida)

That's the reason deacons' sons seldom turn out well, and preachers' daughters are married through a window. [eloped]

An undutiful daughter will prove an unmanageable wife. (1752; Franklin; 1862; Scottish; New Jersey)

Would you know your daughter? Then see her in company.

Daughters-in-Law
A bad daughter-in-law is worse than a thousand devils. (California, New York)

Daughters-in-law become mothers-in-law. (Alaska)

A good daughter makes a good daughter-in-law. (Yiddish)

You speak to the daughter, and mean the daughter-in-law. (Spanish, Yiddish)

NOTES

1. Thiselton-Dyer, *Folklore*, 13–14.
2. Ibid., 240.
3. Rosalind Fergusson, comp., *The Facts on File Dictionary of Proverbs* (New York: Facts on File Publications, 1983), 159.

5

COURTSHIP

Boy meets girl and the proverbs take note of it. Since courtship is an important stage in life, much tradition has built up around the practice. A society's mores and "mating dances" are, therefore, reflected in the sayings of the folk concerning romance.

Six proverbs below treat courtship as a game of chase while others portray it as a contest to be won or lost (A woman must be wooed and won; Boys win girls best with flattery; To win the lady, first bribe her maid). Some proverbs warn about pitfalls, betrayals, and jealousy (Strong men of arms become like putty in the arms of women; A two-faced woman and a jealous man is the cause of trouble since the world began).

Choices can be affected by wealth (A rich man is never ugly in the eyes of a girl; It is as easy to love a rich girl as a poor one) or appearance (Men seldom make passes at girls who wear glasses; The whisper of a pretty girl can be heard further than the roar of a lion; One hair of a woman draws more than a team of horses). These last two proverbs indicate the power of a woman's beauty over a man, which, according to Thiselton-Dyer, is a leading subject of folk wisdom in most countries coupled with a warning that the cost of a woman's beauty leads to a man's empty purse.[1]

So, men are often advised by the proverbs to choose practically by observing the woman when she is working rather than when she is dressed-up and looking her best—after all, one can't judge a book by its cover (Choose a wife on a Saturday rather than on a Sunday; Judge a maiden at the kneading pan, not at the dance). Otherwise, a man might get stuck with a wife "who wants strawberries in January," that is, someone who is frivolous. In addition, a man should "Go down the ladder" when choosing a wife so he can be her superior, but "go up the ladder" when choosing "a friend" so he can advance his social standing.

Generally, men are advised to pursue aggressively (Faint heart never won fair lady; It is a fool who loves a woman from afar) and avoid tramps (A girl worth kissing is not easily kissed) for "a good woman is hard to get and easy to lose." However, should the fickle male be "thrown over," he "usually lands on his knees to another woman."

Following this theme of fickleness, the male double standard is evident in the proverbs: "Gentlemen prefer blondes, but marry brunettes"; men can brag about their sexual prowess, but "A woman who'll kiss and tell is small as the little end of nothing." Inherently, men see commitment as a trap and translate that fear into distrust; thus, they say "A woman would be more charming if one could fall into her arms without falling into her hands"; "Give a woman neither all your love nor all your money." Furthermore, they beg a sympathetic picture: "A woman would sooner rule a heart than fill it; not so a man"; "It is given to women alone to be in love and still retain their self-respect."

Women's calculating image persists (Women do not choose a man because they love him; but because it pleases them to be loved by him; She's got her cap set for him) even though women are considered to be more romantic: "A woman remembers a kiss long after a man has forgotten"; "A young girl never quite gets over her first man" (because it means more to a woman than the "love 'em and leave 'em" man).

Women are warned not to be too choosy (The girl that thinks no man is good enough for her is right, but she's left). Nor should she be too coy. In connection with the proverb "A lass that has many wooers oft fares the worst," Thiselton-Dyer reported: "Many a young girl, we are told, loses her opportunity of marriage through either not being able to make up her mind, or owing to her not being satisfied with one sweetheart."[2] Similarly, concerning "The last suitor wins the maid," "Satirists tell us the folly of believing in a woman's expression of love because it is fickle and unstable."[3] Furthermore, women should try to avoid being foolish (Of all the paths leading to a woman's love, pity is the straightest; Women are apt to see chiefly the defects of a man of talent and the merits of a fool; Women distrust men too much in general and not enough in particular).

Sexist attitudes can be seen in these proverbs. Four use the immature description "girl," but use the adult word "man" for her counterpart. "She likes anything that wears pants" is outdated because of the modern woman's freedom to wear pants, but the saying is still used and reflects the old attitude that pants are unfeminine and for men only.

Despite the maddening messages of some of these proverbs that are sure to inflame the battle of the sexes, overall most people will probably read this set of proverbs and be chagrined by the truthfulness of them, for love is indeed a many splendored and splintered thing.

PROVERBS

General

All women can be caught, spread but your nets.

The best time to select a wife is in the morning. (Vermont)

Boys win girls best with flattery.

But somehow a gal kicks over the milk pail when she lets her ebenezer get up before a feller. [ruins her chances]

Choose a wife on a Saturday rather than on a Sunday. (1659; New Jersey, New York, South Carolina)
   Variation: If you want a neat wife, choose her on a Saturday. (Franklin)
   Variation: Who will have a handsome wife, let him choose her upon a Saturday and not upon Sunday, when she is in her fine clothes.

Choose a wife rather by your ear than your eye. (1866)
   [*See also*: A wife is not to be chosen by the eye only.]

Don't marry a girl who wants strawberries in January. (Ohio)

Faint heart never won fair lady. (1390; California, Illinois, Nebraska)
   Variation: Faint heart never won fair lady . . . or a fat turkey.

Gentlemen prefer blondes—but marry brunettes.

The girl that thinks no man is good enough for her is right, but she's left. (Illinois, Ohio)
   Variation: The girl who thinks no man is good enough for her may be right, but is now often left.

A girl worth kissing is not easily kissed. (Ohio)

Give a woman neither all your love nor all your money. (Mexican-American)

Go down the ladder when you choose a wife; go up when you choose a friend. (1678; Alabama, Georgia, Illinois)

Goodwill, like a good woman, is hard to get and easy to lose. (New Mexico, New York)

If the gal means to git married, her bread will be all dough agin.

If the girls won't run after the men, the men will run after them. (American)

It is a fool who loves a woman from afar. (Indiana)

It is as easy to love a rich girl as a poor one. (1941; New Jersey, New York)

It is given to women alone to be in love and still retain their self-respect.

Judge a maiden at the kneading pan, not at the dance. (Danish; Pacific Northwest)

Kissing a girl because she is willing is like scratching a place that doesn't itch. (Vermont)

A lass that has many wooers oft fares the worst. (1866)

The last suitor wins the maid. (1611; English, French)

A maid that laughs is half taken.

A man chases a woman until she catches him. (California, New York)

Men love women; women love men. (Pacific Northwest)

Men seldom make passes at girls who wear glasses. (1926)

The more a girl runs, the harder a boy chases. (Kansas)

Of all the paths leading to a woman's love, pity is the straightest. (Pacific Northwest)

One hair of a woman draws more than a team of horses. (1591)

A rich man is never ugly in the eyes of a girl. (Illinois)

She likes anything that wears pants. (Washington)

She's flirting like a Spanish filly. (Texas)

She's got her cap set for him. (Texas)

Spring is the time when a young man's fancy turns to what a young woman has been thinking all winter. (1842; New York)

Strong men of arms become like putty in the arms of women.

To win the lady, first bribe her maid.

A two-faced woman and a jealous man is the cause of trouble since the world began. (Wisconsin)

When a woman throws a man over, he usually lands on his knees to another woman. (Mississippi)

When you get one girl you better try two, cause there ain't no telling what one'll do. (Alabama, Georgia)

The whisper of a pretty girl can be heard further than the roar of a lion. (Wisconsin)

A wife is not to be chosen by the eye only. (1797)
   [*See also*: Choose a wife rather by your ear than your eye.]

A wolf is handsome in the eyes of a lovesick girl.

A woman is always grateful to you—for having thrown you overboard. (Pacific Northwest)

A woman is like your shadow; follow her she flies, fly from her, she follows. (Pacific Northwest)
   Variation: Flee and she follows; follow and she'll flee.

A woman must be wooed and won. (South Carolina)

A woman remembers a kiss long after a man has forgotten. (New York)

The woman who confides to one man her partiality for another seeks advice less than avowal. (Pacific Northwest)

A woman who'll kiss and tell is small as the little end of nothing. (New York)

Woman would be more charming if one could fall into her arms without falling into her hands. (1929; Wisconsin)

A woman would sooner rule a heart than fill it; not so a man. (Pacific Northwest)

Women are apt to see chiefly the defects of a man of talent and the merits of a fool. (Pacific Northwest)

Women distrust men too much in general and not enough in particular. (Pacific Northwest)

Women do not choose a man because they love him; but because it pleases them to be loved by him. (Alphonse Karr)

Women love men not because they are men but because they are not women.

A young girl never quite gets over her first man. (North Carolina)

NOTES

1. Thiselton-Dyer, *Folklore*, 25.
2. Ibid., 176.
3. Ibid., 96–97.

6

WOMEN AS PROPERTY

A culture that has traditionally been designed for all things to be classified under the dominion of the male head of a household, and for all things to be seen from the male point of view of higher authority, expresses a male-female relationship in terms of ownership: "Dally not with others' women or money"; "He that lends his wife to dance, or his horse to bullfight, has no complaint to make." The latter proverb means that if harm results, the man has only himself to blame for not keeping his property under his control. However, some possessions are particularly difficult to keep: "After three days men grow weary of a wench, a guest, and weather rainy"; "Arms, women and books should be looked at daily" [a popular German adage that warns a man not to trust a woman further than he can see her]; "Handle with care women and glass."

Until recently, history was written as "his story" with almost all great achievements credited to men and only peripheral attention given to women. For example, our language refers to those who settled the American West as if they were all men—we are told about "the pioneers and their wives and children," which gives no thought to the possibility that the women and children might have been pioneers themselves. Instead, they are considered just part of what came along with the men, like any other part of the baggage or supplies.

In the proverbs, too, when men count up their tangible worth, the women and children are just lumped together with the rest of the goods: "A big wife and a big barn will never do a man any harm"; "A lazy wife and a large barn bring luck to any man"; "There are three faithful friends—an old wife, an old dog, and ready money"; "Three things are as rare as gold: a good melon, a good friend, and a good wife."

Women are often put on a parallel with livestock. For example: "Never pick women or horses by candlelight" (the French say "By candlelight a goat looks like a lady"); "Rooster, horse, and woman should be chosen by breed"; "Manage the horse with the reins, the woman with the spur." Other proverbs found below discuss women in the same breath with mules, poultry, swine, dogs, bees, sheep, and cats.

In like manner, women are connected to sports, games, food, and drink: "Be temperate in wine, in eating, girls, and sloth, or the gout will seize you and plague you both"; "Play, women and wine undo men laughing"; "Wine and women don't mix"; "Wine, women and song will get a man wrong;" "A woman is a dish for the gods"; "Women and wine are the bane of youth"; "Women and wine, game and deceit make the wealth small and the want great."

Men do the proposing, but they act like such put-upon victims and quickly reassign blame if domestic bliss does not ensue. A man is told that he "cannot possess anything better than a good woman, nor anything worse than a bad one," and he certainly knows how to complain about the bad one: "A smoky chimney and a scolding wife are two bad companions"; "I'd as leaf travel as stay home with a scoldin' wife, crying children, and a smoky chimney." Perhaps if he fixed the chimney and tried to please his family he wouldn't have such problems. But, a man is also told "Commend not your wife, wine nor house" "for fear of undue advantage being taken of the confidence reposed in another."[1]

The idea that women are subhuman servants to be counted with the rest of the inventory and disciplined like the family hound is demonstrated by proverbs such as: "My farm troubles me, for a farm and a wife soon run wild if left alone long" and "A woman, a dog, and a walnut tree, the more you beat 'em the better they be." The multitude of variations for this latter proverb is frightening evidence of the prevalence of acceptance for wife-beating in our culture. Current headlines show that many a man still thinks that he can treat his wife any way he wants because she "belongs" to him like a piece of property with which he can do as he pleases. Too many people still think that if a man has to beat his wife to "keep her in line" then it is his right and duty to do so.

If a woman had any great value, then she couldn't be treated so pitifully, but the proverbs tell us "Never run after a woman or a streetcar; there'll be another along in a few minutes." As we see in the section on daughters, the female is an unwanted commodity among humans: "Farmer's luck: bull calves and girl babies," that is, just unusable extras one puts on the market to sell for breeding.

Then again, if the woman is producing she has merit: "A ship under sail and a big-bellied [pregnant] woman are the handsomest two things that can be seen common"; "A little house well filled, a little land well tilled, and a little wife well willed are great riches." Otherwise, a woman is nothing but trouble: "A ship and a woman are ever repairing" (reflecting the many ailments to which, in one form or another, women are supposed to be susceptible[2]); "A barn, a fence, and a woman always need mending"; Swine, women and bees, cannot be turned." Perhaps that is why men pursue other pleasures and hobbies with such fervor. After all, "A woman is only a woman. (A good cigar is a smoke)."

PROVERBS

General

After three days men grow weary of a wench, a guest, and weather rainy. (1733; Franklin)

Arms, women and books should be looked at daily.
  Variation: Arms, women, and locks should be looked at daily. (Wisconsin)

A barn, a fence, and a woman always need mending. (Vermont)

Be temperate in wine, in eating, girls, and sloth, or the gout will seize you and plague you both. (1734; Franklin)

Beware of the forepart of a woman, the hind part of a mule, and all sides of a priest.
  Variation: . . . every side of a priest.

A big wife and a big barn will never do a man any harm.

Children, chickens, and women never have enough. (Wisconsin)

Commend not your wife, wine nor house. (1797; English)

Dally not with others' women or money. (1757; Franklin)

Don't buy a wild horse, nor marry a girl with many boyfriends. (1963; Mexican-American)

Farmers' luck: bull calves and girl babies. (Washington)

Gold, women, and linen should be chosen by daylight. (Wisconsin)

Handle with care women and glass. (1535)
   [*See also*: Women and glass are always in danger.]

He that rides the mule shoes her. [referring to the support of a woman] (1541; New York, South Carolina)

He who lends his wife to dance, or his horse to bullfight, has no complaint to make. (Mexican-American)

I'de as leaf travel as stay home with a scoldin' wife, cryin' children, and a smoky chimney.

A lazy wife and a large barn bring luck to any man. (New York)

A little house well filled, a little land well tilled, and a little wife well willed are great riches. (1735; Franklin; Mississippi, New York, South Carolina)
   Variation: "field" for "land"

Manage the horse with the reins, the woman with the spur. (1963; Mexican-American)

A man cannot possess anything better than a good woman, nor anything worse than a bad one. (Pacific Northwest)

My farm troubles me, for a farm and a wife soon run wild if left alone long.

Never pick women or horses by candlelight.

Never run after a woman or a streetcar: there'll be another along in a few minutes. (Michigan, New York, Pennsylvania)
   Variation: Never run after a woman. They are like streetcars. Stand still, for another one will come along soon. (Vermont)

Play, women and wine undo men laughing. (1670; English)

Rooster, horse, and woman should be chosen by breed. (1963; Mexican-American)

A ship and a woman are ever repairing. (Scottish)
   Variation: A ship and a woman always want trimming.) (1670; English)

A ship under sail and a big-bellied woman are the handsomest two things that can be seen common. ["big-bellied" means pregnant] (1609; 1735, Franklin; English; New York, South Carolina)

A skinny woman's like a racehorse: fast and fun, but no good for work. (New Mexico)

A smoky chimney and a scolding wife are two bad companions. (Illinois)

Swine, women and bees, cannot be turned. (1796)
   Variation: Swine, women and bees, none o' these can ye turn. (Connecticut)

A taught horse, a woman to teach, and teachers practicing what they preach. (1733; Franklin)

There are three faithful friends—an old wife, an old dog, and ready money. (1738; Franklin; Illinois, Indiana, Wisconsin)

There are three things it takes a strong man to hold—a young warrior, a wild horse, and a handsome squaw. (Oklahoma)

Three things are as rare as gold: a good melon, a good friend, and a good wife.

Three things are men most likely to be cheated in: a horse, a wig, and a wife. (1736; Franklin)

Three without rule—A mule, A pig, A woman. (Irish; North Carolina)
   Variation: Three things that will have their way—a lass, a pig, and an ass.
   Variation: The three most difficult to teach—a woman, a pig, and a mule. (English)

To hunt out a wife as one goes to Smithfield for a horse. (1775)

When the wife dies and the mare foals, prosperity begins.

A whistling girl and an old black sheep are the only things a farmer can keep. (North Carolina)
   Variation: A whistling girl and a bleating sheep are the best stock a farmer can keep. (English)

Variation: Whistling girls and jumping sheep are the poorest property a man can keep. (Washington)

Variation: Whistling girls and jumping sheep always come to the top of the heap. (Vermont)

Wine and women don't mix. (Alabama, Georgia)

Wine, women and song will get a man wrong. (1580; English; North Carolina)

A woman, a cat, and a chimney should never leave the house. (Texas)

A woman, a dog, and a walnut tree, the more you beat 'em the better they be. (1581)

Variation: A wife and a walnut tree, the more you beat them, the better they be.

Variation: A spaniel, a woman, and a walnut tree, the more they be beaten, the better they be.

Variation: A woman, a dog, and a hickory tree: the more you beat them, the more they beg.

Variation: A woman, a dog, and a walnut tree: the harder you beat 'em, the better they be. (Texas)

Variation: A woman, a dog, and a walnut tree: the worse you treat them, the better they will be.

Variation: A woman, a spaniel, and a walnut tree, the more you beat them, the better they be.

A woman and a greyhound must be small in the waist. (1866; Spanish)

A woman is a dish for the gods. (New Jersey)

A woman is only a woman. (A good cigar is a smoke.) (California, Michigan, Oregon)

Women and dogs cause too much strife. (1541; Mississippi, New York)

Women and hens are lost by gadding. (Italian; Pacific Northwest)

Women and wine are the bane of youth. (1742)

Women and wine, game and deceit, make the wealth small and the needs great. (1746; Franklin)

Women are ships and must be manned. (Pacific Northwest)

Women, cows, and hens should not run. (North Carolina)

Women, priests and poultry are never satisfied.

NOTES
1. Thiselton-Dyer, *Folklore*, 162.
2. Ibid., 5.

7

BAD WOMEN VERSUS VIRTUOUS WOMEN

This category is different from "Whores and Old Maids" because it does not refer to two particular lifestyles generated by a woman's relationships with men, but rather to the qualities in any woman that evoke disdain or praise. The overall sentiment seems to be that women are always supposed to be virtuous, so a fall from grace is especially damning (Women grown bad are worse than men, because corruption of the best turns to worst; There is nothing better than a good woman and nothing worse than a bad one).

Studies of male/female behavior have shown that women tend to put themselves down and take the blame for whatever goes wrong. Women repeatedly say things such as "I'm sorry" or "Silly me!" or "Wasn't that dumb of me?". On the other hand, men tend to put the blame on other people, never themselves. The worst case example of this behavior occurs when wife-beaters claim that "She made me angry; she made me hit her" while the wife says "It's my fault, I shouldn't have made him angry." Two proverbs follow this line of thinking: "A bad woman will ruin any man" and "If there were not bad women there would be no bad men."

Some men apparently assume that all women are bad (Eve was the only woman without a past; The world is full of wicked women). What makes women so dangerous is their cunning (In craft women can give points to the devil; No woman is too silly not to have a genius for spite; A woman is seldom tenderer to a man than immediately after she has deceived him). As discussed in Chapter 15, on "The Law Under Women," the devil is often associated with women (Having sold her skin to the devil, she bequeaths her bones to God; An ill-tempered woman is the devil's door-mail).

Women are considered bad if they are lazy (A lazy girl and a warm bed are hard to separate; Many estates are spent in getting, Since women for tea forsook spinning and knitting [at least this one adds, "And men, for Punch, forsook hewing and splitting"]). But the most common bad reputation goes to the unchaste woman who "can never become chaste again" and "will hesitate at no wickedness." If being unchaste is so terrible in a woman, why do men keep asking them to be unchaste? It is a paradox—or a hypocrisy—that men insist on a higher standard for women than for themselves; men pressure women into abandoning virtue, yet condemn them vociferously if they do so.

The proverb "The level of the woman is the level of the world" results from the way society has placed the responsibility for the virtue of both men and women on women. "Men are virtuous because the women are; women are virtuous from necessity" is a sad but often accurate explanation of morality: Men are virtuous for the protection of women; women are virtuous out of fear of the consequences (such as pregnancy out of wedlock—the physical evidence won't allow a woman to deny the causative behavior, but until DNA testing came along, a man could deny the charges and get off scot-free).

Similarly, "A woman without religion is a flower without perfume. A man without religion is a horse without a bridle." In this proverb, the woman is not virtuous out of necessity, but is inherently virtuous while the man is naturally amoral and in need of discipline. Many would feel that there is truth in this proverb, too. Both proverbs send the message that, for the sake of making order out of chaos, religion and virtue were instilled into society, but the practice of religion and the enforcement of virtue are often left to the women. A case in point: In a macho society, such as that in Mexico, males are found in church only as boys or old men. In between, they leave religion and virtue to the women; the men stop attending church regularly and engage in promiscuous behavior, even making it standard for a man to have a wife and as many mistresses as he wants. Meanwhile, the wife is expected to accept this situation, forgiving behavior in him that would never be forgiven in her.

Warnings such as "A good girl always gets caught; a bad girl knows how to avoid it"; "Only nice girls blush"; and "So long as woman is on friendly terms with modesty just so long is woman vindicated and no longer" indicate that people are constantly watching lest a woman or girl stray from the straight and narrow. Another admonition would serve well with the "Just Say No" campaign and the renewed call for abstinence: "No padlock, bolts or bar can secure a maiden as well as her own reserve." (Good advice for young men, too.)

While some may not appreciate the value of virtue (An honest woman is no better in his eyes than one of your broomstick jumpers), proverbs send the message that not even beauty, generally considered a woman's strongest asset, can make up for a lack of virtue (Fair woman without virtue is like stale wine).

So virtue is touted in flowery terms as "a star in heaven," "a precious jewel," and "a source of honor." Proverbs further teach "Be a good girl and you will be a true woman" and "Female delicacy is the best preservative of female honor." The rewards of striving for this pristine image are that "Slander expires at a good woman's door" and ". . . roisterers are as quiet as lambs when they fall singly into the clutches of a fine woman."

In proverbs, the parameters for a virtuous woman include knowing that her place is in her house (The best furniture in the house is a virtuous woman; A virtuous woman, though ugly, is the ornament of the house) being subservient to her husband (A virtuous woman commands her husband by obeying him). When such adages are used as part of a girl's education, one has to wonder if the use of proverbs goes beyond moral lessons to the issues of authoritarian standards and control.

PROVERBS

Bad Women

Among 100 men, I have found one good one; among 100 women, not one. (Mexican-American)

A bad woman will ruin any man. (North Carolina)

Better to die by blows than from jealousy fade away. Better to love a dog than a thankless woman, for a dog is grateful when he is fed. (New Mexico)

Cold as a witch's tit.
  Variation: Cold as a witch's titty.
  Variation: Cold as a witch's tit in a brass bra.
  Variation: Cold as a witch's tit at Christmas.
  Variation: Cold as a witch's tit on a windy night.
  Variation: Cold as the nipple on the shady side of a witch's tit.
(North Carolina)

Eve was the only woman without a past.

Fair woman without virtue is like stale wine.

Having sold her skin to the devil, she bequeaths her bones to God.

If there were not bad women there would be no bad men. (1774)

An ill-tempered woman is the devil's door-mail. (Danish; Pacific Northwest)

In craft women can give points to the devil. (Pacific Northwest)

It is easier to find a white crow than a good woman. (1963; Mexican-American)

A jealous woman is worse than a witch.

A lazy girl and a warm bed are hard to separate.

Many estates are spent in getting / Since women for tea forsook spinning and knitting / And men, for Punch, forsook hewing and splitting. (1733; Franklin)

No woman is too silly not to have a genius for spite. (Pacific Northwest)

The unchaste woman can never become chaste again. (Illinois)

The unchaste woman will hesitate at no wickedness. (Illinois)

A woman is seldom tenderer to a man than immediately after she has deceived him. (Pacific Northwest)

Women grown bad are worse than men, because corruption of the best turns to worst. (1866)

The world is full of wicked women. (Ohio)

Good and Bad

A good girl always gets caught; a bad girl knows how to avoid it. (Kentucky, Tennessee)

An honest woman is no better in his eyes than one of your broomstick jumpers.

The level of the woman is the level of the world. (North Carolina)

So long as woman is on friendly terms with modesty just so long is woman vindicated and no longer. (Pacific Northwest)

There is nothing better than a good woman and nothing worse than a bad one. (1948; New York)

A virtuous woman is a source of honor to her husband; a vicious one causes him disgrace. (Illinois)
   Variation: A virtuous woman is a crown to her husband. [Proverbs xii.4 . . . but she that maketh ashamed is as rottenness to his house.]

Virtuous Women

Be a good girl and you will be a true woman. (Pacific Northwest)

Beauty in women is like a flower in the spring, but virtue is like a star in heaven. (1866)

The best furniture in the house is a virtuous woman. (1808; Vermont)

But roisterers are as quiet as lambs when they fall singly into the clutches of a fine woman.

Female delicacy is the best preservative of female honor. (Pacific Northwest)

The honest woman should never believe herself alone. (1963; Mexican-American)

Men are virtuous because the women are; women are virtuous from necessity.

No padlock, bolts or bar can secure a maiden as well as her own reserve.

Only nice girls blush. (Washington)

Slander expires at a good woman's door. (Illinois)

The treasure of a woman is her virtue. (1962; Mexican-American)

A virtuous woman is rarer than a precious jewel. (North Carolina)

A virtuous woman, though ugly, is the ornament of the house. (1866; German)

A woman without religion is a flower without perfume. A man without religion is a horse without a bridle.

8

A WOMAN'S PLACE

Among proverbs can be found many of society's teachings in the past about the place of a woman in a man's world. Definite borders were drawn around a woman to keep her in a tight sphere of duties and expectations, and woe to the woman who tried to step out of bounds. For example, a female should not whistle (When a girl whistles, the angels cry). There are actually over a dozen variations of the proverb "A whistling girl and a crowing hen" (although only six are shown here because some have only a slight change of wording, thus, to save space and avoid minute repetition, only important changes are shown; see Mieder's dictionary for more), indicating that the "boyish" activity of whistling was considered as out of character for a girl as a hen crowing. One suspects that the proverb also expresses an underlying fear that if girls do whistle, then maybe somebody besides the rooster could rule the roost. Such a possibility could not be tolerated, so girls had to be restricted by tight codes of conduct to keep them from exploring areas that men wanted to keep to themselves.

This same theme of crowing hens also expresses a fear that the cock will be silenced entirely: "It is ill with the roost when the hens crow and the cock must remain silent." Men have taken this example from the barnyard in an attempt to make it seem as unnatural a reordering of position for women to have a say as it is for hens to crow. We know it doesn't happen with hens, so why should it happen with females of another species? Despite the reputation given to women of being talkative (see chapter 9, "Talkativeness"), when it comes to authoritative speech, men should do the talking and women should listen (The noblest sight on earth is a man talking reason and his wife listening to him).

Besides, "What a woman has to say above a whisper isn't worth listening to." Of course, she has to be kept uneducated for that proverb to remain true. Again, the barnyard provides the analogy: "A mule that whinnies and a woman that talks Latin never come to any good." One has to wonder if the examples from the livestock reflect an attitude that men considered women to be on the same level (see chapter 6, "Women as Property"). At any rate, the whisperings of a demure response to a command and pillow talk, not intellectual discourse, are all men wanted to hear from women because "A man doesn't want a woman smarter than he is," so "A wise woman never outsmarts her husband." She is told not to deliberate or calculate or she will be lost because she just doesn't have the head for it. If indeed she does have intelligence, then she is "twice a fool"—once for being a woman in the first place and twice for having a talent she can't use.

The lesson is that there are rules of placement: "Men build houses; women build homes"; "Nature framed women to be won, and men to win." Just as the rooster rules the roost, human males should rule the world (Let not the maid become the mistress). Women shouldn't "meddle" with politics because "Women in the Senate House are like monkeys in a glass ship." Fame for a woman would be the "tomb of her happiness" because "A woman's place is in her home" and surely going outside of it would make her miserable (or is it him?).

Thus, "Women have no rank." Although this proverb can mean that women have no authority and no right to it, this proverb also holds true concerning management styles. Men insist on a hierarchy, and their egos have them constantly jockeying for higher positions; their ambition and identity is validated by power and titles. Women in the traditional world, however, saw themselves as all being in the same boat, and the bonds of sisterhood felt on occasions such as childbirth, seeing loved ones off to war, or just coping with men superseded artificial positioning. Today this lack of ranking is seen in the leadership style of women, which tends more to manage with group input than "top-down" dictates. Women can't understand all the fuss about "Total Quality Management" because that is the way they have always governed. It is a sad joke that suddenly men are getting excited about, writing books about, and getting paid high consulting fees for a system that women have always used and would have been practiced in business a long time ago if women had been allowed to participate.

The topic of several proverbs is concerned with the wearing of breeches or trousers. While now out-of-date, wearing pants was once a practice so closely tied with male identity and authority that no lady would ever dare be caught wearing them (Ladies in slacks should not turn their backs; When ladies wear the breeches, their petticoats ought to be long enough to hide 'em), even if one author admits disapprovingly that it would be just as "nateral." Prohibiting women from wearing this male symbol was a visual way to separate them and another way to restrict their movement.

"Ladies first" applied only if the lady made herself presentable by not smoking, not asking questions, and not showing pride. Not that there was much opportunity to go first or go anywhere since "a woman's work is never done"—probably because perpetual labor would keep her "out of mischief." I am reminded of a male visitor we once had in our home from Pakistan. He was fascinated with all of our kitchen appliances. His wife lived in purdah and cooked over an open fire in the middle of the compound. My mother asked him if it wouldn't be nice for her to have such conveniences to make her work easier. He replied, "Oh no! Then she would have time to get into trouble!"

Even a compliment could be turned into a restriction: "Behind every great man there is a great woman" may be intended to give the woman some credit in the success of her man, but it still says that the success is his, not hers, and that she should be not beside him, but back behind him in a supportive-only role, quiet and unseen. A woman is told that she "can't drive her husband" (translated: she shouldn't be a nag), "but she can lead him." The problem is that the proverb is not advising that she be in front of him taking charge, only that, in a woman's nurturing way, she can guide him to the fulfillment of *his* potential.

"Women are necessary evils" who were "placed on earth to show men both paradise and purgatory." But first the earth belonged to the men, and the only way to endure this other but lesser half of the equation was to get them under control with restrictions. The woman or girl who did not abide by the dictums governing her sex was a misfit, a fish out of water, an unnatural occurrence. To avoid rebellion, men were advised that "Women, like gongs, should be beaten regularly" and that would keep them in their place.

PROVERBS

General

As for politics, I don't believe wimmen have any right to meddle with them, more than a cat wants trousers.

Behind every great man there is a great woman. (Mississippi)

Custom has given woman petticoats and man pantaloons, but it would be just as nateral for woman to wear the breeches and man the apronstrings, and there is a plaguy sight of them do it too.

It is ill with the roost when the hens crow and the cock must remain silent. (Texas)

Keep the ladies busy and that keeps them out of mischief. (1908; New York, South Carolina)

Ladies don't smoke. (North Carolina)

Ladies first.

Ladies in slacks should not turn their backs. (Oregon)

Let not the maid become the mistress. (1784)

Little girls shouldn't ask questions.

A man doesn't want a woman smarter than he is. (North Carolina)

Man works from sun to sun, But woman's work is never done. (1570; New York, North Carolina,)
   Variation: A man works from dawn to setting sun, but a woman's work is never done. (1866)
   Variation: Man's work lasts till set of sun; woman's work is never done.
   Abbreviated Variation: A woman's work is never done. (1570)
   Variation: A woman's work is never at an end. (1866)

Measure that woman . . . for a pair of breeches; she's determined to wear 'em.

The men and dogs for the barn, the women and cats for the kitchen. (California)

Men build houses; women build homes. (1938)

A mule that whinnies and a woman that talks Latin never come to any good.

Nature makes women to be won, and men to win. (Illinois)
   Variation: Nature framed all women to be won.

The noblest sight on earth is a man talking reason and his wife listening to him. (Texas)

A proud woman brings distress on her family. (Cingalese; Illinois)

She wears the trousers. (Yiddish)

What a woman has to say above a whisper isn't worth listening to. (New Jersey)

When a girl whistles, the angels cry. (New York)

When ladies wear the breeches, their petticoats ought to be long enough to hide 'em. (New York, South Carolina)

A whistling girl and a crowing hen always come to some bad end. (1721; Scottish; California, Louisiana, North Carolina)
   Variation: A whistling woman and a crowing hen are two of the unluckiest things on earth.
   Variation: A whistling woman and a crowing hen are neither fit for God nor men. (English)
   Variation: A whistling girl and a cackling hen come to no good end. (New Mexico)
   Variation: Girls who (that) whistle and hens that crow should have their necks twisted betimes.
   Variation: A whistling girl and a crowing hen, are sure to come to some bad end. (Texas)
   Variation: The girl that whistles or a hen that crows always catch the nicest beaux. (Nebraska)

A wise woman is twice a fool.

A wise woman never outsmarts her husband. (Kansas, New York)

Woman at her housework: that's what women are for. (Mexican-American)

A woman can't drive her husband, but she can lead him. (New York)

A woman's fame is the tomb of her happiness. (Pacific Northwest)

A woman's place is in the home. (1844)
   Variation: A woman's place is in the hay.
   Variation: Woman's sphere is in the home.

The woman that deliberates is lost. (1713; New Jersey)
   Variation: The woman that "calc'lates" is lost.

Woman was placed on earth to show men both paradise and purgatory.

Women are necessary evils. (1547; Latin; Illinois)

Women have no rank.

Women in the Senate House are like monkeys in a glass ship.

Women, like gongs, should be beaten regularly.

9

TALKATIVENESS

One of the characteristics consistently attributed to women is that of being talkative (Generally speaking, woman is generally speaking). Legend has it that "Ten measures of talk were sent down from heaven, and women took nine." As a result, "The best of women is never at a loss for words," and "When women are on board there is no want of wind."

As a symbol of talkativeness, a woman's tongue is the subject of twelve of the proverbs listed below. We are told that a woman's tongue is long and sharp as well as active, and as such it can be a potent weapon. The proverb "A squaw's tongue runs faster than the wind's legs" is evidence that this observation about women extends across cultures.

Chattering is bound to lead to gossip, and women do indeed have a reputation for being terrible gossips (Wherever there is a woman, there is gossip). Despite this proverb, modern research has shown men to be the worse gossips (One proverb concedes: Men gossip as much as women do, but not so meanly). Related to gossip is the inability to keep a secret (A woman can never keep a secret), or so five proverbs below claim.

Studies have also shown that women are more adept at communication in general. While, on average, men are better in areas such as depth perception and mathematics, women consistently score higher in language skills. Women are also more expressive of their emotions, so the result is that women are much more likely to talk than men. Better communication abilities should be a valued talent, but in the male-dominated world, the difference in women was not to be appreciated, but rather to be ridiculed. The proverbs reflect this lack of understanding.

But the act of talking is perhaps not the real bone of contention. Rather, it is a matter of power and control. In chapter 11, "Flightiness," there is a discussion concerning the way men constantly interrupt women in conversation because they want to be in control of the discourse and don't think women have anything to say that is worth listening to anyway. Underlying the lack of respect is, in actuality, a fear that women truly might have something important to say (The conversation of a woman is worth all the libraries in the world). In that case, men would have to share leadership. To prevent such a turn of events, men developed the philosophy that "A woman has never spoiled anything with silence." So, all this complaining about a woman's talkativeness is really a way of trying to silence them altogether: Create a myth that women talk too much and you have a perfect right to tell them to shut up.

Real life shows women being told to be quiet, having their voices silenced by omission from the dialogues of power, and having their needs ignored. It's a neat trick to claim that women talk a lot while refusing to allow them to be heard. Perhaps that is why they talk so much: Keep trying and maybe one day you'll get through. Perhaps, too, it should occur to the world that if women were allowed to join in where it counts, there wouldn't be a need to verbalize their frustrations at length among themselves.

PROVERBS

General

Any woman can keep a secret, but she generally needs one other woman to help her. (Mississippi)

The best of women is never at a loss for words. (Pacific Northwest)

Blessed is the woman who can keep a secret and the man who will not tell his wife. (Mississippi)

The conversation of a woman is worth all the libraries in the world. (Wisconsin)

Generally speaking, woman is generally speaking. (Vermont)

Her tongue moved like a clapper in a cowbell. (North Carolina)

It is not the nature of the female tongue to be silent. (1792)

A man-servant knows more than he tells; a maid-servant tells more than she knows.

Men gossip as much as women do, but not so meanly. (Pacific Northwest)

One tongue is enough for two women. (1732)

The only secret a woman can keep is that of her age. (1732; Kentucky, Tennessee)

Silence is a fine jewel for a woman, but it is little worn. (1539; Irish; Illinois)
    Variation: "veil" for "jewel." (1795)

A squaw's tongue runs faster than the wind's legs. (Oklahoma)

Talking women sound like chickens eating scratch feed on a tin roof. (North Carolina)

Tell a woman and you tell the world. (1700)

Ten measures of talk were sent down from heaven, and women took nine.
    [*See also*: Women have nine measures of talk.]

/Three women and a goose make a market. [noisy] (1866)
    Variation: Three men and one hog make a market. (1866)
    [*See also*: Where women and geese are there is no lack of noise.]

When a woman is speaking, listen to what she says with her eyes. (New York)

When women are on board there is no want of wind. (American)

Wherever there is a woman, there is gossip. (West Virginia)

Where women and geese are there is no lack of noise. (English; Pacific Northwest)
    [*See also*: Three women and a goose make a market.]

A woman always thinks it takes two to keep a secret.

A woman can never keep a secret.
    Variation: "cannot" for "can never"

A woman fights with her tongue.

A woman has never spoiled anything through silence. (German)

A woman never holds her tongue: but when she's contriving mischief. (1720)

A woman's hair is long; her tongue is longer. (Oregon)

A woman's strength is in her tongue. (1659; English; Ohio)

A woman's tongue is only three inches long, but it can kill a man six feet high. (Japanese)

A woman's tongue is sharper than a double-edged sword. (Vermont)

A woman's tongue wags like a lamb's tail.

Women have nine measures of talk. (Yiddish)
    [See also: Ten measures of talk were sent down from heaven and women took nine.

Women's tongues are made of aspen leaves. (1747)

10

WHORES AND OLD MAIDS

The expression "You're damned if you do and damned if you don't" certainly applies to whores and old maids in proverbs. Among the proverbs about whores, contradiction abounds. Is it "As hard as a whore's heart" or "As soft as a whore-lady's heart"? "Once a whore" is it "always a whore" or is "A young whore, an old saint"?

The acceptance of the existence of prostitution as if it were inevitable (It's a poor family that has neither a whore nor a thief in it) allows the subject of brothels to be used as a routine and raunchy analogy (More commotion than a whorehouse on Saturday night; To smell like a whorehouse on Saturday night).

But the shrugging acceptance of the business of prostitution doesn't mean acceptance of the person in society. It is another example of the double standard that men create the demand for prostitutes, but are the first to condemn them to the lowest station. To say that a whore is solemn, ultrapolite, demure, nervous, or obvious at a christening is to say that she has no place in a holy church because of her sinful life. Whores are an abomination, a reverse of the ideal of the virtuous woman. Therefore, their curses are blessings and spittle is like rain to them because everything in their lives is a rejection of what should be.

Prostitution is a tragic way of life resulting from another way that women are used by men. An underlying recognition of the unfairness of the position into which some women are put is perhaps the reason for sayings such as "As long as a whore's dream"—so many of the good things in life have been denied a prostitute that her life leaves a lot to be desired. Sympathy for her plight or guilt about her treatment has created a common mythology that portrays a prostitute as a basically good

woman who took a wrong turn, and allows the perpetuation of charac-
ters like Belle Watley in *Gone With the Wind* or the Julia Roberts role in
Pretty Woman. However, for most prostitutes there is no glamor, no
kindly Horace as in *Dr. Quinn* to marry them and make them respectable. There will be no "old saint" who just had an adventuresome youth
like an old man who sowed his wild oats when he was young. Prostitution is not a profession that women choose freely or enjoy, and it is
therefore a sick distortion to pretend that there's "nothing dirty goin' on
'round here" (*Best Little Whorehouse in Texas*). For women, "whoring
around" is no lark but is a life of violence and degradation that many do
not survive.

The disdain for harlots is as old as the profession, but the criticism of
celibacy developed out of the Protestant Reformation as a reaction to the
Catholic emphasis on the sanctity of the celibate life, especially within
religious communities. So determined were Protestants to distance themselves from this Catholic philosophy that emphasis was put on the necessity of marriage to the extent that unmarried women were considered
a subject worthy of ridicule.

Evidence of this ridicule can be found in a widely played card game
that trains little minds early to be afraid of ending up as the "Old Maid."
Being the old maid is something to be feared because proverbs tell us
that old maids are particular and peevish and have stinging tongues, and
that without a man a woman is sour and desperate (I have an idea that
gall will either die a sour old maid or have to take a crooked stick for a
husband at last; Prouder than an old maid with a new feller) and all dried
up (As dry as an old maid's lips).

Old maids are rejects (Always a bridesmaid, but never a bride; Left to
dance in a hog trough [said of a girl who has been jilted or of an older
sister whose younger one has married before her]). Whether they were
not chosen for marriage partners because they were ill-natured or
whether they become ill-natured because of being an old maid is not
clear, but legend has it that "Old maids lead apes in hell" "where the
old batchelors are turn'd to apes." Supposedly, the only use for which
an old maid is suited is to command a vulgar lower life form in hell,
although if that is what old bachelors become in hell, the single life for
men is apparently not given much respect either.

Since an old maid "doesn't know anything but what she imagines,"
she might think she knows something about raising children even though
she has none of her own (Bachelor's wives and maid's children are well
taught; Old maids fancy nobody knows how to bring up children but
them).

This category—and those of sex, courtship, place, property, wives, and
widows—demonstrate that society has viewed women not holistically,

but only in terms of their sexual nature and their relationship with men. But with all the baggage (described in these categories) that comes with men, perhaps it is true that "It takes a wise woman to be an old maid."

PROVERBS

Whores

As cold as a whore's heart. [*In Sanskrit literature*: There is no oil in the lantern, just as there is no affection in a courtesan.]
   Variation: As hard as a whore's heart.

As long as a whore's dream.

As soft as a whore-lady's heart.

As solemn as a whore at a christening. (1754)
   Variation: As polite as a whore at a christening.
   Variation: He looked as demure as a harlot at a christenin'.
   Variation: Nervous as a whore in church.
   Variation: Nervous as a pregnant prostitute in church.
   Variation: Stand out like a whore at a christening.

It's a poor family that has neither a whore nor a thief in it. (1566; New York, South Carolina)

More commotion than a whorehouse on Saturday night.
   [*See also*: To smell like a whorehouse on Saturday night.]

Once a whore, always a whore. (1613; English; Illinois)

Spit in a whore's face and she'll say it's raining. (Illinois)

To smell like a whorehouse on Saturday night.
   [*See also*: More commotion than a whorehouse on Saturday night.]

Whores curses are blessings (1855; English; Illinois)

A young whore, an old saint. (English)

Old Maids

Always a bridesmaid but never a bride. (1954)
   Variation: Always a maiden, never a wife.
   Variation: If you are three times a bridesmaid, you will never be a bride.
   Variation: If you serve three times as a bridesmaid, you'll never marry.
   Variation: Often a bridesmaid but never a bride.
   Variation: Three times a bridesmaid, (but) never a bride.

As dry as an old maid's lips.

As particular as an old maid. (Texas)

As peevish as an old maid. (1728)

Bachelor's wives and (old) maid's children are well taught. (1795; Pacific Northwest)

I have an idea that gall will either die a sour old maid or have to take a crooked stick for a husband at last.

It takes a wise woman to be an old maid. (New York)

Left to dance in a hog trough. [said of a girl who has been jilted or of an older sister whose younger one has married before her]

An old maid doesn't know anything but what she imagines. (Vermont)
   [*See also*: What a woman does not know she imagines.]

Old maids fancy nobody knows how to bring up children but them. (1546; English; Nebraska, New York, North Carolina, South Carolina)

Old maids lead apes in hell. (1735; Franklin)
   Variation: Old maids lead apes there, where the old batchelors are turn'd to apes. (1735; Franklin)

Prouder than an old maid with a new feller.

Thorns and thistles sting very sure, but old maids' tongues sting more.

11

FLIGHTINESS

Cheris Kramer wrote in her article "Folk Linguistics: Wishy-Washy Mommy Talk" that "Compared to male speech, the female form is supposed to be emotional, vague, euphemistic, sweetly proper, mindless, endless, high-pitched, and silly."[1] It follows then that, if women's speech is so flighty, women are flighty and fickle themselves (As changeable as a woman). We have a body of folklore that portrays women with this image, and proverbs do their part to maintain the caricature.

The main element of the image is that women change their minds all the time ("It's a woman's privilege to change her mind" and several others). A tragic consequence of this image is the supposition by men that if a woman can't make up her mind, then a man should make her decisions for her. Not only does this supposition follow the male-domination theory, it allows men to excuse rape with the oft-repeated "She wanted it, too." What really happened is that the man decided for the woman that she wanted sex just because he did, and then he justifies his thinking with the reinforcement he got from proverbs such as "Girls say no when they mean yes" and "A woman will refuse and then accept." A woman's "no" can mean "yes" because she is probably just being silly and coy. Throw in the double standard and you get "When a lady says no, she means perhaps; when she says perhaps, she means yes; when she says yes, she is no lady."

Part of the reputation of being flighty involves being seen as unreliable (Women are as fickle as April weather), wasteful (A woman could throw out with a spoon faster than a man could throw in with a shovel), opportunistic (Trust your dog to the end, a woman to the first opportunity), and dumb (What a woman doesn't know she imagines). On top of that, a woman is notoriously frivolous (The exercise a woman likes most is running up bills; It never occurs to a fashionable woman that there is enough goods in the train of her dress to make a poor child a Sunday frock.) From the proverb "The man earns and the woman spends" we get not only the message that a man is responsible and the woman is a spendthrift, but also a message about place—the nature of who does what in the scheme of things. Men run things and women run around on whim needing no reason for what they do (Because is a woman's excuse; A woman's in pain, a woman's in woe; a woman is ill when she likes to be so).

Proverbs tell us that women should be classified with the wind and weather (It's a fact that's indisputable; women, like winds, are very mutable; Winter weather and women's thoughts change often; Woman is as variable as a feather in the wind; Woman is a weathercock; Women's clocks will walk with every wind). Maybe someday "women will be harmonized" and not so hard to figure out; until then, "man does not know woman, but neither does woman."

Such proverbs take a terrible toll on women's efforts to be taken seriously. If "You can never pin a woman down to an answer," then "There's no accounting for the actions of women" and they can be easily dismissed. However, recent analyses of women's speech patterns and their interactions with men in conversation may explain this appearance of flightiness and help women to correct the problem. Women try so hard to please others that they will back off or change to be agreeable. But as women learn to be more assertive and assume more positions of authority, their insecure nature will be replaced with more confidence and an improved image of reliability.

PROVERBS

General

As changeable as a woman. (English; North Carolina)

Because is a woman's excuse. (Nebraska)

Between a woman's yes and a woman's no, There's not enough room for a pin to go. (English, German, Russian, Spanish; North Carolina)
   [See also: Girls say no when they mean yes.]

The exercise a woman likes most is running up bills.

Girls learn faster than boys and forget easier. (Pacific Northwest)

Girls say no when they mean yes.
  Variation: A woman's "no" means "yes." (Nebraska)
  Variation: When a lady says no, she means perhaps; when she says perhaps, she means yes; when she says yes, she is no lady. (1594, Shakespeare; New York, North Carolina, South Carolina)
  Variation: A lady says no, meaning maybe, and maybe, meaning yes; but when she says yes, she isn't a lady.
  [*See also*: Between a woman's yes and a woman's no, There's not enough room for a pin to go.]

Inconstant as a woman's love. (1803)

It is a thing that's indisputable; Women, like winds, are very mutable. (1748)

It never occurs to a fashionable woman that there is enough goods in the train of her dress to make a poor child a Sunday frock. (Pacific Northwest)

It is a woman's privilege to change her mind. (1616; Michigan, New York, South Carolina)
  Variation: Every woman has the divine privilege of changing her mind.
  Variation: Ladies have leave to change their minds.
  Variation: To change the mind is a lady's privilege. (1500; English; New York, South Carolina)
  Variation: A woman may change her mind.

Like a gal's mind, no two minits alike.

The man earns and the woman spends. (Italian)

There's no accounting for the actions of women.

True man does not know woman, but neither does woman.

Trust your dog to the end, and a woman to the first opportunity.

What a woman does not know she imagines.
  [*See also*: An old maid doesn't know anything but what she imagines.]

When the stars fall agin maybe the women will be harmonized. [Therefore, never.]

Winter weather and women's thoughts change often. (1450; Illinois)

A woman could throw out with a spoon faster than a man could throw in with a shovel. (New York)
   Variation: A wasteful woman throws out with a spoon faster than her husband can fetch in with a shovel. (North Carolina)
   Variation: A wasteful wife throws out in the dishwater more'n her husband can tote in. (North Carolina)
   Variation: She threwed more out the backdoor than her old man could tote in the front. (North Carolina)
   Variation: A woman can throw away more [food] with a spoon than a man can bring in with a shovel. (Indiana)
   Variation: A woman can throw out more with a spoon than a man can bring home with a shovel. (Vermont)

A woman don't know her own mind half an hour together. (1771)

Woman is as variable as a feather in the wind.

Woman is a weathercock (turning vane). [unsteadfast] (English)

A woman's excuses are like her apron, easily lifted. (English; North Carolina)

A woman's in pain, a woman's in woe; a woman is ill when she likes to be so. (Italian; North Dakota)

A woman will refuse and then accept. (1733)

Women are as fickle as April weather. (German; Illinois)

Women's clocks will walk with every wind. (North Carolina)

You can never pin a woman down to an answer. (North Carolina)

NOTE

1. Cheris Kramer, "Folk Linguistics: Wishy-Washy Mommy Talk," in *Exploring Language*, 3rd ed., ed. Gary Goshgarian (Boston: Little, Brown and Company, 1983), 253.

12

SEX

Since sex has been a taboo subject until recent times, there are not very many proverbs that dare to discuss it. However, in their own way, proverbs get the message across, and the predominant message seems to be that chastity is a pretense of women (Chaste is she whom no one has asked; Modesty is a quality in a lover more praised by a woman than liked) that is easily cast aside (Neither a fortress nor a maid will hold out long after they begin to parley). Once virtue has been abandoned, through guilt or justification, "The cheating wife doubts the chastity of all women."

Men are known to be preoccupied with sex ("Women and glass are always in danger" is a reference to the difficulty of maintaining chastity under this constant bombardment of demand[1]), and they assume that women feel the same way that they do. This transference causes the man to create or use a proverb that paints a woman to be as lustful as he is ("A bag of fleas is easier to keep watch over than a woman" and "A girl, a vineyard, an orchard, and a beanfield are hard to watch" are references to keeping watch over a woman's chastity[2]), thereby giving him an excuse for his behavior. Besides, she needs sex or she'll end up "tough ez wire."

Using a woman for sex, any woman (after all, "All women look the same after the sun goes down"), is a governing behavior according to the tone of "Every Jack has his Jill, if one won't another will" and "No prison is fair, no mistress foul." T. F. Thiselton-Dyer says in his *Folklore of Women* that this latter proverb means that beauty is deceptive, especially where love is concerned.[3] This interpretation coincides with the Illinois variation, "There are no ugly loves nor handsome prisons," but more is probably involved here than the blindness of love. Lust dictates that any woman will do for sex, even ugly ones, because the man is not, at that point, as interested in her face and figure as he is in other body parts.

Making a woman useful is a primary occupation for a man, although he doesn't want to make her useful for someone else (An old man marrying a young girl is like buying a book for someone else to read). If a man puts some time into the effort, he discovers "Keep a mistress seven years and you'll find her as useful as a wife" referring, of course, to the provision for a common-law wife. And it's never too late to start, for "Old maids make good lovers." This last proverb results from the myth that old maids, having been deprived of sex for so long, will have a store of pent-up passion and, thus, will go crazy with sex when given the chance.

The double standard applies to women as loose as the men with the aforementioned attitudes. Such women are ridiculed (She was pure as the snow, but she drifted; She won't do it with anybody but a friend— and she ain't got an enemy in the world; The impatient virgin becomes a mother without being a bride). Immorality has its rewards, though, because, while "every wench [may have a] sweetheart, the dirtiest [will have] the most."

The game of sex has certain rules: "If you can kiss the mistress, never kiss the maid," meaning don't risk losing the better deal. Once the man has that first kiss, though, "the rest come easy" because, to repeat, a woman isn't as virtuous as she pretends. Let her put up a good front for appearances, but persevere and you'll soon know if "she do" or "she don't."

Only one proverb of those below upholds the image of virtue as a natural characteristic of a woman: "Women at lust are a contradiction." Overall, the proverb-makers believed that "A woman never forgets her sex. She would rather talk to a man than an angel any day," implying that she would always rather be engaged in pillow talk than working on her virtue.

PROVERBS

General

A bag of fleas is easier to keep watch over than a woman. (German) [*See also*: A girl, a vineyard, an orchard, and a beanfield are hard to watch.]

Chaste is she whom no one has asked. (1695; Illinois)

The cheating wife doubts the chastity of all women. (Illinois)

Every Jack has his Jill, if one won't another will. (Nebraska, New York)
  Variation: There is a Jack for every Jill. (California)
  Variation: There's no Jack without a Jill; if one won't, another will.
(Vermont)

Every wench has her sweetheart, and the dirtiest the most.

Getting kisses out of a woman is like getting olives out of a bottle; the
first may be devilish difficult, but the rest come easy. (New York, Ohio,
South Carolina)
  Variation: Kissing a girl for the first time is like getting the first olive
from a jar: after the first one, they come rolling out. (Oklahoma)

A girl, a vineyard, an orchard, and a beanfield are hard to watch. [One
has to worry about what might get stolen or given away.]
  [*See also*: A bag of fleas is easier to keep watch over than a woman.]

A girl's first man (affair) is never forgotten.
  Variation: A woman never forgets her first love.

If you can kiss the mistress, never kiss the maid.[don't risk losing the
better deal] (1659; Texas, Wisconsin)
  Variation: Never kiss the maid, if you can kiss the mistress.

The impatient virgin becomes a mother without being a bride.

Keep a mistress seven years and you'll find her as useful as a wife.

Modesty is a quality in a lover more praised by a woman than liked.
(Illinois)

Neither a fortress nor a maid will hold out long after they begin to
parley. (Franklin)

No prison is fair, no mistress foul. (French)
  Variation: There are no ugly loves nor handsome prisons. (Illinois)

Old maids make good lovers. (An old hen makes a good stew.)
(Mexican-American)

An old man marrying a young girl is like buying a book for someone
else to read. (New York, Vermont)

She was pure as the snow, but she drifted. (New York)

She won't do it with anybody but a friend—and she ain't got an enemy in the world. [said of a girl with loose morals] (1944; Indiana)

Some say she do, and some say she don't.

Virgins uv forty-five . . . tough ez wire.

A woman never forgets her sex. She would rather talk to a man than an angel any day. (1872; Wisconsin)

Women and glass are always in danger.
    Variation: A woman and a glass are never out of danger.

Women at lust are a contradiction. (North Carolina)

NOTES

1. Thiselton-Dyer, *Folklore*, 12.
2. Ibid.
3. Ibid., 30.

13

WIDOWS

Of greatest surprise, perhaps, among the proverbs about women is the way widows are treated. Despite the ethic that society must look after widows and their children (Befriend the widow and fatherless), society apparently does so with a jaundiced eye (He that marries a widow and four children marries four thieves).

This attitude arises from the popular myth that women are conniving golddiggers (The rich widow cries with one eye and rejoices with the other), an opinion developed by a culture in which men largely control the money and women are put in the position of having to earn wealth and power by means other than employment—that is, through men.

In that light, too, a woman without a man, such as a widow, has no identity or purpose (A widow is a boat without a rudder). Note as Robin Lakoff did in her article "You Are What You Say" that "The woman whose husband dies remains 'John's widow'; John, however, is never 'Mary's widower.' "[1] (A widow is known by her weeds, a man for his deeds).

Without a husband, the woman becomes a burden on the rest of the family; it is assumed that she cannot take care of herself, and the resentment of the duty boils over into some nasty remarks about the temperament and usefulness of widows (There are three classes of people one must not provoke: officials, customers, and widows; The widow gave orders to her cat and the cat gave them to its tail [runaround]). Having a widow in the family, then, is a sticky situation in that the family must graciously take on an added responsibility while secretly harboring a desire to see her unloaded on another husband quickly (Modesty becomes a virgin, but it's a vice in a widow). Of course, if the widow is rich, the task becomes easy (Rich widows are the only second-hand goods that sell at prime cost).

Marrying a widow is a big risk for a man according to the proverbs. It will cost him either a lot of money (He that marries a widow with two daughters has three back doors to his house) or a lot of grief if he is compared to the first husband (He that marries a widow will often have a dead man's head thrown into his dish; Never marry a widow unless her first husband was hanged).

If the first marriage was not a pleasant one, though, the death of a mean or distant husband might bring more relief than grief (One sorrow drowns another: yesterday my husband died, and today I lost my needle; Onions can make ev'n heirs and widows weep), particularly if the widow is young enough to enjoy her new freedom (The three merriest things under the sun: A cat's kitten, A goat's kid, And a young widow). She might then go on a hunt for a husband more suitable and of her own choosing (Widows who cry easily are the first to marry again. There is nothing like wet weather for transplanting; A girl receives—a widow takes, her husband; You can't marry a widow, for the widow marries you). Or she might choose to remain in and enjoy her respectable and independent status (Widows will be widows).

The proverbs on widows are something of a shock, yet upon reflection one realizes that it is a fairly accurate representation of society's opinion that a woman was meant for marriage and the guardianship of a husband. Outside of marriage, either by death or divorce, a woman has no one to keep her in line. Many proverbs teach that women are inherently bad (see chapter 7, "Bad Women versus Virtuous Women"), so when turned loose they will become loose (Hotter than a grass widow's kiss). Such stereotyping is always a mistake. The world needs to learn to let people be themselves without labels, assumptions, or categories. Being a wife, a mother, or a widow is not an all-consuming occupation or identity; it is just one aspect of a woman's life and her relationships with others.

PROVERBS

General

Befriend the widow and fatherless. (Michigan)

A girl receives—a widow takes, her husband.

He that marries a widow will often have a dead man's head thrown into his dish. (1802; English, Spanish)

Variation: . . . unless he has been a widower, then it is tit for tat.

He that marries a widow with two daughters has three back doors to his house. [It's expensive.] (English, Scottish; North Carolina)

He who marries a widow and three children marries four thieves. (Danish; Pacific Northwest)
  Variation: He that marries a widow and four children marries four thieves. (1576; New York)

Hotter than a grass widow's kiss. [A grass widow is a divorcée.]

Modesty becomes a virgin, but it's a vice in a widow.

Never marry a widow unless her first husband was hanged. (1721; Celtic, Scottish; Wisconsin)

One sorrow drowns another: yesterday my husband died, and today I lost my needle. (New York)

Onions can make ev'n heirs and widows weep. (1734; Franklin; New York)

The rich widow cries with one eye and rejoices with the other. (1866) (Mexican-American, "smiles" for "rejoices")
  Variation: A rich widow weeps with one eye and laughs with the other. (Portuguese)

Rich widows are the only second-hand goods that sell at prime cost. [attributed to Franklin] (Texas)

There are three classes of people one must not provoke: officials, customers, and widows.

The three merriest things under the sun: A cat's kitten, A goat's kid, And a young widow. (Irish; North Carolina)

The widow gave orders to her cat and the cat gave them to its tail. [runaround]

A widow is a boat without a rudder. (Chinese)

A widow is known by her weeds [clothes], a man for his deeds.

Widows who cry easily are the first to marry again. There is nothing like wet weather for transplanting. [Attributed to Oliver Wendell Holmes] (Texas)

Widows will be widows. (American)

You can't marry a widow, for the widow marries you. (New York)

NOTE

1. Robin Lakoff, "You Are What You Say," in *Exploring Language* 3rd ed., ed. Gary Goshgarian (Boston: Little, Brown and Company, 1983), 251.

14

OLD WOMEN AND GRANDMOTHERS

Reference to old women in proverbs is often made more for an analogy than a criticism or description (The morning rain is like an old woman's dance, soon over). Explaining a process often involves personification, and the clichéd choice for a person could be an old woman if the process is somehow associated with an old woman's work (It's like the old woman's soap—if it don't go ahead, it goes back; It takes two old women to make a cheese: one to hold and the other to squeeze; The old woman is picking her geese [it's snowing]).

Also among proverbs is a suggestion that a woman's temperament becomes difficult and demanding with old age (As fussy as an old woman; The old ladies interfere, and make you walk right straight up to the chalk, whether or no; Old wives and children make fools of physicians). Perhaps "The hell of women is old age" because it is believed that women fall apart and lose their looks (Old houses and old ladies always need repairing), thus depreciating their value, unless they have money or the security of marriage (Old woman's gold is not ugly; As comfortable as matrimony . . . to an old woman). If there is not money, then "Need [will make] the old wife trot."

The branch of old women known as grandmothers is full of dear souls to be revered; therefore, proverbs find them a good subject when trying to depict how despicable some people can be based on how they treat the beloved grandma (So dishonest he'd steal his grandmother's false teeth; Mean enough to steal the pennies from his Grandmother's eyes [referring to the practice of putting coins on the closed eyes of a dead person to keep them shut]; He would sell his grandmother for a buck). In contrast, those who know that Grandma is too sweet a soul for anyone to wish harm would say "I couldn't . . . no more than I could strike my granny" or would understand that a situation would have to be extremely maddening to be "enough to make a Quaker [known for adherence to nonviolence] kick his grandmother."

It may not be too exciting to spend time with Grandma (Dull as an evening with grandma), but one had best heed her counsel and not try to act smart around her (Don't teach your grandmother how to milk ducks or suck eggs). This reverence of grandmothers in contrast to disdain for old women is perhaps a reflection of human nature: We are fond of those we know and fear those we don't, forgetting that the old lady we don't know is probably somebody's grandmother.

The Ojibway tribe of North America have a good way of tying the present and the future together with the expression "The grandfathers and the grandmothers are in the children; teach them well," meaning that the wisdom and traditions we respect in our elders had its beginnings in the way they were reared, so if we want their descendants to develop the same traits, we must be careful with their upbringing. The future is now.

PROVERBS

Old Women

As comfortable as matrimony . . . to an old woman. (Illinois)

As fussy as an old woman.

The hell of women is old age. (1948; Kentucky)

It's like the old woman's soap—if it don't go ahead, it goes back.

It takes two old women to make a cheese: one to hold and the other to squeeze. (Maine)

The morning rain is like an old woman's dance, soon over. (English, German; North Carolina, Texas)
   Variation: A morning's rain is like an old woman's dance: it doesn't last long. (1640; Mississippi, South Carolina)

Need makes the old wife trot. [akin to: "Money makes the mare go."] (1225; English; Oklahoma, Texas)

Old houses and old ladies always need repairing.
   [*See also*: A ship and a woman always need repairing.]

The old ladies always interfere, and make you walk right straight up to the chalk, whether or no.

Old wives and bairns [children] make fools of physicians. (1721; Scottish; New York)

The old woman is picking her geese. [Old woman = Mother Nature; It is snowing.] (English; North Carolina)

Old woman's gold is not ugly. (1732; Wisconsin)
   Variation: An old female's gold is never ugly.

Grandmothers

Don't teach your grandmother how to milk ducks or suck eggs. (1707; South Carolina, Texas)
   Variation: Do not try to teach your grandmother how to suck eggs.

Dull as an evening with grandma. (Washington)

The grandfathers and the grandmothers are in the children; teach them well. (Ojibway)

He would sell his grandmother for a buck. (North Carolina)

I couldn't . . . no more than I could strike my granny.

It's enough to make a Quaker kick his grandmother.

Mean enough to steal the pennies from his Grandmother's eyes.

So dishonest he'd steal his grandmother's false teeth. (Washington)

15

THE LAW UNDER WOMEN

What if women ruled? Opinion varies among the proverbs as to what would happen, but there is a dire warning that feminine rule would be terrible indeed: "Better the devil's than a woman's slave." In fact, surely the devil would have to be involved in a situation so unnatural (When a woman reigns the devil governs; When the wife rules the house, the devil is man-servant; Woman rules man, but de debil rules her). After all, "There's hardly a strife in which a woman has not been a prime mover" and "There never was a conflict without a woman."

Nonetheless, a couple of proverbs admit that, although we may give lip-service to male governance, it is probably women who actually rule (As the good man saith, so say we; but as the good woman saith, so must it be; The husband is the head of the house, but the wife is the neck— and the neck moves the head). Others concede outright that women rule (It is said that when a woman wets her finger, fleas had better flee; Two things govern the world—women and gold; What woman wills God wills; Where there's a world it's woman that will govern it). But this rule is perhaps more one of sentiment than substance that is connected to the universal devotion and submission to mothers (The hand that rocks the cradle rules the world).

Two proverbs pertain to issues discussed in chapter 8, "A Woman's Place." "Let the women wear the breeches" once again refers to the symbolism of authority that pants used to carry. "There is little peace in that house where the hen crows and the cock is mute" brings up the same analogy of the unnatural state of crowing hens as "Whistling girls and crowing hens always come to some bad end."

At least the rule of women is given some credit for promoting a refined civilization (Ladies will sooner pardon want of sense than want of manners; The society of ladies is a school of politeness). In fact, one proverb asserts "Women leave peace behind 'em when they go," and the hope is that, as women assume more and more positions of leadership in the world, this saying will prove true.

PROVERBS

General

As the good man saith, so say we; but as the good woman saith, so must it be. (1866)

Better the devil's than a woman's slave.

The hand that rocks the cradle rules the world. (1881)

The husband is the head of the house, but the wife is the neck—and the neck moves the head. (North Carolina)
    Variation: Man is the head, but woman turns it.

It is said that when a woman wets her finger, fleas had better flee.

Ladies will sooner pardon want of sense than want of manners. (1866)

Let the women wear the breeches. (1564; Mississippi)

The society of ladies is a school of politeness. (1866)

There is little peace in that house where the hen crows and the cock is mute.

There's hardly a strife in which a woman has not been a prime mover. (1658; Illinois, Oregon)

There was never a conflict without a woman.

Two things govern the world—women and gold. (Oregon)

What woman wills God wills. (French; Pacific Northwest)

When a woman reigns the devil governs. (Italian; Pacific Northwest)

When the wife rules the house, the devil is man-servant.

Where there's a world it's woman that will govern it.
  Variation: "While" for "Where" (Illinois)

Woman rules man, but de debil [devil] rules her. (Indiana)

Women leave peace behind 'em when they go. (1906; New York)

16

A WOMAN AND HER HOUSE

This chapter is a short one, but the fact that a collection of proverbs on the relationship of a woman and a house can be made at all is an important indication of traditional expectations about a woman's place (A woman's place is in the home; see chapter 8). Today, many people think that "Most women are better out of their houses than in them." But the old world told a woman that she was to be in the home (A woman, a cat, and a chimney should never leave the house; see chapter 6) and her job was that of housewife, a word to be used synonymously with wife. Therefore, young women were warned that "Where the cobwebs grow, the beaux don't go," meaning that men won't marry those who do not have the requisite domestic skills.

Since housekeeping was the only occupation for a woman, her success at keeping house established her reputation (You know a good house-keeper by her windows). Reinforcing the (house)work ethic, women were told that "A nurse spoils a good housewife"; "While the tall maid is stooping the little one has swept the house"; and "The more women look in their glass the less they look in their house"—so don't be lazy or vain. Thiselton-Dyer reported that the cynicism of the proverb-makers was not complimentary to the charms of the fair sex. Beautiful women had the reputation of being less handy and serviceable than plain ones.[1]

The link between a woman and her house was so much a part of her identity that the furnishings of the house could determine her personality and temperament (Bare walls make gadding wives; A house well-furnished makes a good housewife). In addition, the household animals could play a part in the job: "Between a cross dog and a cross-eyed woman, a house is well kept; he barks and she swings the broom"; "The eye of the housewife makes her cat fat" (a sharp-eyed housewife would direct the cat to mice and other edible varmints; on the other hand, if she is sloppy enough to attract rats and such, the cat will also eat well: "When the housewife is a slattern, the cat is a glutton").

Even though some women could make their home an unpleasant place to be (It is better to dwell in the corner of a housetop than with a brawling woman in a wide house), somebody had to do the housekeeping. So, everything in the home could fall apart if the woman was not up to the task (House goes mad when women gad) or if there were no woman at all (A house without a woman and firelight, is like a body without soul or sprite; A house without a woman is like a boat without a rudder; You can't keep house with a dead woman [probably said to a widower to encourage him to marry again]).

But as bad or worse than no woman would be two women for "No house was ever big enough for two women" and "Two women in the same house can never agree." In response to these two proverbs, one has to ask what else could be expected: Limit a woman to one occupation only and she is bound to be territorial. If the message of the proverbs is that there is nothing else for a woman but service in the home, then she shouldn't be asked to share her only source of power. But such a worry is less a consideration today when women have many spheres of influence, and their lives and the lives of those around them are the richer for it.

PROVERBS

General

Bare walls make gadding wives. (1866)
Variation: Cold walls make unhappy wives. (Irish; North Carolina)

Between a cross dog and a cross-eyed woman, a house is well kept: he barks and she swings the broom.
Variation: A cross-grained woman and a snappish dog take good care of the house. (Danish; Pacific Northwest)

The eye of the housewife makes her cat fat. (Illinois)

House goes mad when women gad. (1822; Kansas, Wisconsin)

A house well-furnished makes a good housewife.

A house without a woman and firelight, is like a body without soul or sprite. (1733; Franklin; American, New York, South Carolina)

A house without a woman is like a boat without a rudder. (Italian)

It is better to dwell in the corner of a housetop than with a brawling woman in a wide house. (1948; Alabama, Georgia)
   Variation: It's better to live on the top of the house than with a contentious woman. (Vermont)

The more women look in their glass the less they look in their house.
   [akin to: "The more a woman admires her face, the more she ruins her house." (Spanish)]
   Variation: The more women look in their glass, the less they look to their houses. (1866; English)
   Variation: The more women look in their glass the less they look in their hearts. (1796)
   [*See also*: The wife who loves the looking-glass hates the saucepan.]

Most women are better out of their houses than in them. (Pacific Northwest)

No house is big enough for two women. (Oriental; California)
   Variation: "was ever" for "is" (1450; Maryland, Mississippi)
   Variation: No home large enough for two women to manage.
   Variation: Two women cannot live under one roof.
   [*See also*: Two women in the same house can never agree.

A nurse spoils a good housewife. (1659; English; Illinois)

Two women in the same house can never agree. (1417)
   Variation: Two women in one house, two cats and one mouse, two dogs and one bone, will never accord.
   [*See also*: No house is big enough for two women.]

When the housewife is a slattern, the cat is a glutton. (Yiddish)

Where the cobwebs grow, the beaux don't go. (New York, Texas, Vermont, Washington)

While the tall maid is stooping the little one has swept the house. (1866)

You can't keep house with a dead woman. (Pennsylvania Dutch)

You know a good housekeeper by her windows. (Vermont)

NOTE

1. Thiselton-Dyer, *Folklore*, 27.

17

MISCELLANEOUS

So many of the proverbs listed elsewhere in this collection could have fit under more than one category, and then there were those that didn't seem to fit anywhere quite right. Consequently, a miscellaneous category was created for this eclectic, but very interesting, group. These are not mere leftovers; they are unique.

A few are obviously modern: "Backbone is what a woman shows in modern gowns," "A career girl would rather bring home the bacon than fry it," and "A woman should hang on to her youth, but not while he's driving."

Several are addressed directly to men or are spoken by men, once again assuming a male point of view: "An aversion to women is like an aversion to life"; "Do right and fear no man; don't write and fear no woman"; "I would have a woman as true as Death"; "The only difficulty in being able to read women like a book is that you are liable to forget your place"; and "The woman you keep keeps you."

Among this potpourri is the silly (Men never learn anything about women, but they have a lot of fun trying), the superstitious (Never trust a red-headed woman), the chauvinistic (Nothing will ruin an interesting intellectual conversation any quicker than the arrival of a pretty girl), and the snide (Three kinds of men can't understand women: young men, old men, and middle-aged men).

In 1774, surely this country was too new (it wasn't even independent yet) for people to be making judgments about our culture, yet from that time there is the saying "No women indulged like the American." Maybe all that indulgence is compensation for emotional pain: "Men's fortunes and women's hearts stand a great deal of breaking."

There is one proverb here that is quite disturbing: "If one woman were to tell the truth about her life, the whole world would split open." We are told that most rapes and beatings are never reported. Now that women are being encouraged to come forward and to reveal the truth, we are being stunned with the extent of the violence. Women have been silenced or have kept quiet out of fear throughout history in most societies (Men's hearts are full of deceit, and women are their confiding victims). Women finally telling the truth about their lives is perhaps also an explanation for the modern turmoil associated with the women's movement. Once women started speaking up, everything began to change, from roles to clothes.

Finally, one of this author's favorite proverbs: "Women are men with better clothes." The author begs forgiveness for bringing levity into the conclusion of this collection, but "A woman's wit is a help."

PROVERBS

General

Any wise man can be fooled by a foolish woman. (New York)

An aversion to women is like an aversion to life. (New York)

Backbone is what a woman shows in modern gowns.

A career girl would rather bring home the bacon than fry it.

Do right and fear no man; don't write and fear no woman. (1450; Illinois, Indiana, New York)

Every girl has her day. (Kentucky, Tennessee)

Everyone can tame a shrew but him that has her. (1866)

Far-fetched and dear bought, is good for the ladies. [meaning a bargain] (1350; Michigan)

Fire dresses the meat, and not the smart lass. (1866)

Fools are wise men in the affairs of women. (1866; New York)

Girls think men are all soul; women know they are all stomach. (Pacific Northwest)

A girl with cotton stockings never sees a mouse. [those who could afford cotton stockings would not likely encounter vermin.]

A good surgeon must have an eagle's eye, a man's heart and a lady's hand. (1585; Illinois, Indiana, New York,)
   Variation: A good surgeon must have an eagle's eye, a lady's hand, and a lion's heart.

If a woman drowns hunt her upstream. (Pacific Northwest)

If one woman were to tell the truth about her life, the whole world would split open.

It's a woman's maxim, "False in a small degree, false in every degree."

I would have a woman as true as Death.

A lady is a woman who makes it easy for a man to be a gentleman. (Illinois)

The last generation will be female.

Men never learn anything about women, but they have a lot of fun trying.

Men's fortunes and women's hearts stand a great deal of breaking.

Men's hearts are full of deceit, and women are their confiding victims. (1866)

Never trust a red-headed woman. (Washington)

Nothing will ruin an interesting intellectual conversation any quicker than the arrival of a pretty girl. (New York)

No woman likes to hear her male friends ridiculed. (Pacific Northwest)

No women indulged like the American. (1774)

The only difficulty in being able to read women like a book is that you are liable to forget your place.

The proof of gold is fire; the proof of woman, gold; the proof of man, woman. (1733; Franklin)

Variation: Gold is tested with fire, a woman with gold, and a man with a woman. (New York, Vermont) [akin to: "Gold is tested by fire, men by gold." (1666; Italian)]

There is somethin' wus than galls in bushes.

Three kinds of men can't understand women: young men, old men, and middle-aged men.

To go through (something) like a dose of salts through a woman
  Variations: "Hired girl" or "tall Swede" for "a woman" (Illinois)

A truth-telling woman finds few friends. (Danish; Pacific Northwest)

Twice is a woman dear; when she comes to the house and when she leaves it. (Pacific Northwest)

The woman always pays.

Woman: God bless her by that name, for it is a far nobler name than lady. (1931; New York)

Woman is a mystery to men but women are wise to each other. (Illinois)

A woman should hang on to her youth, but not while he's driving. (North Dakota)

The woman to whom you give what she asks for, is the woman who will give you what you ask for. (1962; Mexican-American)

A woman's wit is a help.

The woman you keep keeps you. (Illinois)

Women are men with better clothes.

18

CONCLUSION

"To what extent do proverbs reflect tension, perhaps otherwise unexpressed and hidden, in the culture itself? Are these phrases not a common-denominator clue to the state of mind of a given group?"[1] So asks Joseph Raymond in his article "Tensions in Proverbs," and it is a question that must be asked here. Are American proverbs about women a clue as to the state of mind of the American people? They certainly could be.

In the introduction to the *Prentice-Hall Encyclopedia of World Proverbs*, Wolfgang Mieder asks similar questions: "Do the proverbs of the old country still fit all aspects of modern American life? Does only the older generation use them, and how do the young people react today to this ethnic wisdom?" Mieder's answer fits the hypothesis of this work: "Each individual is . . . to a certain degree preprogrammed by the traditional proverb stock that continues to be handed down from generation to generation. At the same time, new proverbs are still being added to this repertoire. . . . While such new proverbs are added to our basic stock, older ones may drop out since they no longer reflect newer attitudes."[2]

Given the preponderance of proverbs in this collection that are noted to have been used for hundreds of years, one has to wonder if outmoded proverbs are dropping out fast enough. Even the modern proverb "A career girl would rather bring home the bacon than fry it" is rife with sexist bias: The use of "girl" instead of "woman" indicates the patronizing attitude that women should be treated like children and not given respect or recognition as adults. The implication is that bringing home the bacon is a rejection of the expected role of housewife.

Nonetheless, the point is made that new proverbs can be made and old ones eliminated as they lose their suitability. An examination of American proverbs about women might help speed the process along if it raises the consciousness of the reader. It often takes pointing out a problem to people before they realize that one exists and can then take action about its solution. This book is an effort to do that pointing out by saying that the problem is that a disturbing number of the American proverbs about women are derogatory. These proverbs are full of sexism, satire, and bitterness. With the assumption that proverbs do still teach each generation their culture, these proverbs are then detrimental to the progress of women's fulfillment.

While Neal Norrick has said that data on the use and effect of the proverb is rare (see "Introduction"), there is evidence from related areas that justifies the logical assumption that sexist proverbs have a sexist influence in personal relationships and in the work place. In *Words and Women*, Casey Miller and Kate Swift reported that

> Jill Volver, a Justice Department lawyer who became prominent as an assistant prosecutor during the Watergate trials, put the situation this way: "If I were to act like a man in a courtroom, the jury wouldn't accept me—yelling and shouting, as some of the lawyers in the Watergate case did, are not acceptable in women. It's far more effective for me to be quiet and ask questions than it is for me to get in a fight with a witness." Both more effective with a jury and with the rest of society that insists her role as a woman must take precedence over her role as an attorney. Men are not required to make a similar choice.[3]

Where did this attorney learn her code of conduct? According to Dwight Bolinger in an essay entitled "Truth Is a Linguistic Question": "Women are taught their place . . . by the implicit lies that language tells about them." Bolinger makes the same argument as this book that "linguists and others should show more concern not only with the way language is used—and with questions of appropriateness—but also with the way language *is*—and with questions of the fitness of language to the perceptions of the speakers."[4]

Following that line of thinking, Jennifer Williams and Howard Giles in their essay "The Changing Status of Women in Society: An Intergroup Perspective" reported that "one strategy women are using today is to refuse to accept the negative definition of themselves that has been organized and perpetuated by men. Women concerned with language cull dictionaries, fiction, and conversations for the terms used to define women, in order to document the type and extent of the linguistic putdown of women."[5]

Certainly, that is the strategy behind this work, and it is done with the same intent stated by Ruth Todasco in her introduction to the *Feminist English Dictionary*. Todasco urges open discussion of the words created by a male-dominated society (for example, the many epithets for women) so that their power can be defused: "a general awareness of their sexism can weaken their authority" and thus promote the spread of ways of speaking that do not devalue women.[6]

This need to ferret out the sexist offenses in language arises from the problem that so much of what people say results from a less-than-conscious effort. "Consciousness raising" is not just a trendy phrase; it is a necessary campaign. As Miller and Swift reminded us: "Ready-made phrases, as George Orwell said in his essay "Politics and the English Language" are the prefabricated strips of words and mixed metaphors that come crowding in when you do not want to take the trouble to think through what you are saying. 'They will construct your sentences for you,' he said, '—even think your thoughts for you, to a certain extent—and at need they will perform the important service of partially concealing your meaning even from yourself.' "[7]

McConnell-Ginet, Borker, and Furman provide a marvelous summary of the problem described by Orwell as it is manifested in sexist language:

> No one, of course, maintains that language is the *only* influence on people's ways of thinking or that a person can achieve all her or his desired social ends armed only with linguistic resources. But it is in part because the connections of language to thought and to social life are seldom explicitly recognized that language use can enter into the transmission and preservation of attitudes and values that are seldom explicitly articulated. Many—probably most—of our linguistic choices in ordinary conversation are not consciously reflected upon. This means that many of the messages we convey and receive are "loaded" with import beyond their overt content and perhaps beyond what the speaker intended. Overt messages are, of course, important but they do not raise any interesting theoretical questions. Any husband can say to his wife: "I'm the boss around here." Any child may hear "you're just a dumb broad" often enough to come to believe that it must be an apt characterization. Such open grabs for power and blatant expressions of misogyny are always possible and can, of course, have tremendous impact. Yet it is the covert messages that are most difficult to resist, that we may unwittingly send ourselves, and that are easiest for the dominant group (sometimes sincerely) to deny.[8]

The mention in this quote of what a child might hear is very important to this discussion. The point made all along is that language influences our perceptions of the world. This influence begins with the very first words a child hears and continues throughout a child's absorption of speech patterns and vocabulary as the formative years go by. If we know that language programs children, then we can reasonably say that language, and its elements such as proverbs, is a powerful determiner of social values. There are studies such as that of Joyce Penfield and Mary Duru in "Proverbs: Metaphors That Teach" that "suggest how the metaphorical and quotative nature of proverbs contributes to the process of child development in daily interaction in oral societies."[9] Since all children start out in what is a strictly oral society for them, the influence of language is largely the same on their early development whether they are born into a Nigerian tribe or American suburbia.

As McConnell-Ginet, Borker, and Furman surmised:

> Language may be effective in socializing newcomers to traditional ways of viewing the world in part because they assume it is an index of values and attitudes. . . . So long as the child's inferences aren't obviously contradicted by (nonlinguistic) experience or by the bulk of the overt content of people's utterances she or he can assume that "this is how people think around here." It doesn't even matter if most of the adults consciously accept the values attributed to them by children: the child may incorporate as basic assumptions a variety of principles that powerfully influence later behavior and beliefs and which can only be rooted out with great difficulty, thus insuring the continued influence of cultural belief systems that have long since been rejected at a conscious level by large cultural subgroups.
>
> We still know virtually nothing about this process, but it is important to realize that we need not suppose that our language-learning experience determines what we think in order to say that patterns of language use encountered by children contribute substantially to forming their way of viewing themselves and their world.[10]

One would think that since the above essay was written in 1980 that progress would have been made in learning about this process, and surely there has been since the connection of language and thought is of great concern to researchers of late. Yet in 1990 Kenneth Dion was still asking:

> To what extent do parents and teachers employ proverbs as socialization devices? If they are employed, how effective are they compared to other socialization tactics aimed at shaping children's behaviour, such as reasoning, and so on? Are single parents perhaps more apt to rely on proverbs in socializing their children? Do proverbs play a role in fostering ethnic identification in children? Are we more apt to pass on to our own children those proverbs we have heard from our parents, as Page and Washington found in a sample of single, black American mothers? These and other interesting questions await answers.[11]

One of the interesting questions awaiting an answer is the one raised by this book concerning American proverbs about women. As a groundbreaking work, this reference book is just a start—it is the question itself coupled with an attempt at an answer. The response to this work may be the actual answer. Once people see these proverbs about women gathered together as a body, what will be the reaction? Will readers be simply amused or truly alarmed by the proverbs? Critics such as Deborah Cameron say that the problem is not the words but the meaning behind the words. This author does not see a conflict between Cameron and word-choice reformers like Miller and Swift. Hasn't connotation always been more important than denotation? But isn't it easier to eliminate the words with negative connotations than to convince a society to change the meaning?

Certainly changes can occur as has been seen with many words about women that started out innocently (for example, mistress and spinster), but took on perverse meanings over time as the result of the manipulation of an antifemale society that had a long list of reasons for making feminine authority or things feminine undesirable. Perhaps a profemale society could turn meanings around again. But how is a profemale society achieved? Well, perhaps some of the words, phrases, and proverbs that hinder society from thinking positively about women have to be changed. Obviously, the argument can go around and around. Perhaps anything done that is positive and fair would help.

It is the intent of this book to intrigue others with this topic enough to begin investigating on their own. In 1992, Hiroko Storm did a similar study about "Women in Japanese Proverbs." The abstract reads:

By examining proverbs about women one can see to some extent how women are perceived in a certain culture. This paper discusses traditional Japanese proverbs about women, as well as newer sayings that appeared after World War II. It then presents the results of a questionnaire survey on such proverbs. The survey, which sought to clarify contemporary Japanese attitudes on women, indicated which of the eighteen proverbs on the questionnaire were considered to describe women correctly and which incorrectly; it also showed how the image of Japanese women differs from that of women in general, and what influence the respondent's age and gender have on his or her views.[12]

It is interesting to note here that Storm accepts proverbs as cultural indicators and that Storm came up with basically the same category choices that are used in this book:

1. Women in general: a. inferiority; b. stupidity; c. changeability; d. ill-nature; e. talkativeness; f. weakness; g. miscellaneous

2. Women in specific roles or situations: h. wives; i. mothers-in-law and daughters-in-law; j. widows; k. prostitutes; l. intelligent women; m. beautiful women.[13]

The more scholars investigate this subject in particular, the more will be known about how much proverbs determine the mindset of American culture in general. It should be noted also that the author understand that her interpretations of this collection are not the only ones possible. Other opinions are certainly valid and welcome since they will contribute to the body of discussion about the weight of proverbs when it comes to the image of women. Furthermore, other approaches to the study of these proverbs is possible. When examining social elements, it is always interesting to look at the impact of mores and religious attitudes of certain periods. With that in mind, these proverbs could be categorized according to images such as woman as madonna, woman as Eve or Magdalene, woman as nurturer or childlike dependent, and so on. How have these images changed over time and how has that change been reflected in the proverbs? On a broader scale, how does the picture change as one compares proverbs about women from one country to the next?

It has been established that, in the past, the creation of proverbs has been largely the responsibility of male authors. On top of that, most of the folklore scholars have been male. How, then, has the view of women portrayed in proverbs been distorted by male prejudice or the positive aspects of womanhood been ignored because women have not had their own say? That question must be part of the study now that the days of absolute male dominance are over in the United States, and women can bring their own point of view to the examination of language and folklore.

NOTES

1. Joseph Raymond, "Tension in Proverbs: More Light on International Understanding," *Western Folklore* 15 (1956): 153.

2. Wolfgang Mieder, *Prentice-Hall Encyclopedia of World Proverbs: A Treasury of Wit and Wisdom Through the Ages* (Englewood Cliffs, NJ: Prentice-Hall, 1986), x–xi.

3. Casey Miller and Kate Swift, *Words and Women* (Garden City, NY: Anchor Press/Doubleday, 1976), 108.

4. McConnell-Ginet, Borker, and Furman, *Women in Language*, 66.

5. Ibid., 62.

6. Ibid.

7. Miller and Swift, *Words and Women*, 151.

8. McConnell-Ginet, Borker, and Furman, *Women in Language*, 7–8.

9. Joyce Penfield and Mary Duru, "Proverbs: Metaphors That Teach," *Anthropological Quarterly* 61.3 (1988): 119.

10. McConnell-Ginet, Borker, and Furman, *Women in Language*, 8.

11. Kenneth L. Dion, "Psychology and Proverbs," *Canadian Psychology* 31.3 (1990): 210.

12. Hiroko Storm, "Women in Japanese Proverbs," *Asian Folklore Studies* 51.2 (1992): 167.

13. Ibid., 168–69.

ALPHABETICAL INDEX
OF PROVERBS

A page number in bold brackets following each proverb indicates that proverb's location in this book.

Afoot and alone, as the gal went to be married. **[30]**
   Taylor and Whiting, p. 152, #3.
After three days men grow weary of a wench, a guest, and weather rainy. **[69]**
   Franklin, 1733.
All are good girls, but where do the bad wives come from? **[22]**
   (*Variation*: All are good lasses; but where come the ill wives frae?)
   Mieder, Dic., p. 251, #5, New York.
   (Loomis, GE, p. 197, #13.) (1866) (Scottish) (Spanish)
All brides are child brides in their mother's eyes. **[30]**
   Mieder, Dic., p. 70, #3, New York.
All married women are not wives. **[22]**
   Kin, p. 185.
All painted and varnished up as neat and shining as one of your New York gal's faces on a Sunday. **[47]**
   Taylor and Whiting, p. 126, #1.
All women and cats are black in darkness. **[36]**
   Mieder, Dic., p. 666, #33, Wisconsin. (1745, Franklin)
All women are good; good for something or good for nothing. **[36]**
   Brown, p. 111.
   Loomis, GE, p. 197, #14. (1866) (English)
All women can be caught, spread but your net. **[63]**
   Kin, p. 174.

All women look the same after the sun goes down. **[36]**
  Emrich, p. 67.
  Mieder, Dic., p. 666, #34, Illinois. (1948)
Always a bridesmaid, but never a bride. **[31]**
  (*Variation 1*: Always a maiden, never a wife.)
  (*Variation 2*: If you are three times a bridesmaid, you will never be a bride.)
  (*Variation 3*: If you serve three times as a bridesmaid, you'll never marry.)
  (*Variation 4*: Often a bridesmaid but never a bride.)
  (*Variation 5*: Three times a bridesmaid [but] never a bride.)
  Mieder, AP, p. 92, Pennsylvania. (no "but")
  Mieder, Dic., p. 70. (1954)
  (1. Brunvand, Dic., 91.)
  (2, 3, 4, 5. Mieder, Dic., p. 70.)
Always sweep where your mother-in-law looks. **[56]**
  Mieder, AP, p. 88, New Mexico.
The American woman, if left to her own devices, washes on Monday, irons on Tuesday, bakes on Wednesday and marries on Thursday. **[36]**
  Brunvand, Dic., p. 3.
Among 100 men I have found one good one; among 100 women, not one. **[77]**
  West, p. 43, Mexican-American.
Any girl can handle the beast in a man if she's cagey enough. **[36]**
  Mieder, Dic., p. 251, #6, Mississippi.
Any wise man can be fooled by a foolish woman. **[120]**
  Mieder, Dic., p. 661, #21, New York.
Any woman can keep a secret, but she generally needs one other woman to help her. **[88]**
  Mieder, Dic., p. 667, #36, Mississippi.
Arms, women, and books should be looked at daily. **[69]**
  (*Variation*: "locks" for "books"
  Kin, p. 14.
  (Mieder, Dic., p. 27, #2, Wisconsin.)
As changeable as a woman. **[96]**
  Whiting, PPNC, p. 345, North Carolina. (English)
As cold as a whore's heart. **[93]**
  (*Variation*: As hard as a whore's heart.)
  Taylor, PCSC, p. 28. [Taylor reports that in Sanskrit literature it is said "There is no oil in the lantern, just as there is no affection in a courtesan."]
As comfortable as matrimony . . . to an old woman. **[108]**
  Barbour, p. 296, #55, Illinois.
As dry as an old maid's lips. **[94]**

Taylor and Whiting, p. 233, #2.
As flat as a bride's biscuits. [31]
    Taylor, PCSC, p. 41.
As for politics, I don't believe wimmen have any right to meddle with
them, more than a cat wants trousers. [83]
    Taylor and Whiting, p. 61, #54.
As fussy as an old woman. [108]
    Taylor, PCSC, p. 43.
As great a pity to see a woman weep as to see a goose go barefoot. [36]
    Mieder, Dic., p. 667, #37. (1523)
As long as a whore's dream. [93]
    Whiting, MPPS, p. 681.
As particular as an old maid. [94]
    Atkinson, p. 90, Texas.
As peevish as an old maid. [94]
    Whiting, EA, p. 273, M7.
As soft as a whore-lady's heart. [93]
    Taylor, PCSC, p. 28.
As solemn as a whore at a christening. [93]
    (*Variation 1*: As polite as a whore at a christening.)
    (*Variation 2*: He looked as demure as a harlot at a christenin'.)
    (*Variation 3*: Nervous as a whore in church.)
    (*Variation 4*: Nervous as a pregnant prostitute in church.)
    (*Variation 5*: Stand out like a whore in church.)
    Whiting, EA, p. 481, W141. (1754)
    (1 and 5. Whiting, MPPS, p. 682.)
    (2. Taylor and Whiting, p. 172, Harlot.)
    (3. Person, p. 184, #296.)
    (3 and 4. Clark, p. 172, #692, North Carolina.)
As the good man saith, so say we; but as the good woman saith, so it
must be. [112]
    Brown, p. 109.
    Loomis, GE, p. 197, #49. (1866)
At a wedding feast, the one to eat the least is the bride. [31]
    Brown, p. 18. (Spanish)
An aversion to women is like an aversion to life. [120]
    Mieder, Dic., p. 666, #35, New York.
Bachelor's wives and maid's children are well taught. [94]
    (*Variation*: Old maids [and bachelors] are experts on child care.)
    Hines, p. 110, Pacific Northwest.
    Loomis, FA, p. 173. (1795)
    Taylor, WMWO, p. 4. (old maid's)
    (Whiting, MPPS, p. 392.)
Backbone is what a woman shows in modern gowns. [120]

Brown, p. 113.
A bad daughter-in-law is worse than a thousand devils. [58]
  Mieder, Dic., p. 135, #1, California, New York.
A bad wife likes to see her husband's heels turned to the door. [22]
  Hines, p. 285, Pacific Northwest. (Danish)
A bad wife ruins a family. [22]
  Mieder, AP, p. 54. (Chinese)
A bad woman will ruin any man. [77]
  Whiting, PPNC, p. 345, North Carolina.
A bag of fleas is easier to keep watch over than a woman. [100]
  Kin, p. 275. (German)
Bare walls make gadding wives. [116]
  (Variation: Cold walls make unhappy wives.)
  Loomis, GE, p. 197, #47. (1866)
  (Whiting, PPNC, p. 492, North Carolina.) (Irish)
A barn, a fence, and a woman always need mending. [69]
  Mieder, Dic., p. 38, #1, Vermont.
  Mieder, TLSM, p. 52, Vermont.
Be a good girl and you will be a true woman. [79]
  Hines, p. 167, Pacific Northwest.
Beauties without fortunes have sweethearts plenty, but husbands none
at all. [47]
  Loomis, GE, p. 197, #20. (1866)
Beauty in women is like a flower in the spring; but virtue is like a star in
heaven. [79]
  Loomis, GE, p. 197, #22. (1866)
"Because" is a woman's excuse. [96]
  Welsch, p. 266, Nebraska.
Befriend the widow and fatherless. [104]
  Mieder, Dic., p. 652, #1, Michigan.
Behind every great man there is a great woman. [83]
  Mieder, Dic., p. 267, #2, Mississippi.
  Titelman, p. 22.
The best-dressed woman usually arrives with the least. [47]
  (Variation: The best-dressed woman usually arrives last with the
least.)
  Mieder, Dic., p. 667, #60.
The best furniture in the house is a virtuous woman. [79]
  Loomis, FA, p. 176. (1808)
  Loomis, GE, p. 196, #2. (from Robert B. Thomas' Farmer's Almanack,
1808.) [a house]
  Mieder, Dic., p. 243, #1, Vermont.
  Mieder, TLSM, p. 51, Vermont. [a house]
The best of women is never at a loss for words. [88]

Hines, p. 293, Pacific Northwest.

The best time to select a wife is in the morning. [63]

Mieder, TLSM, p. 51, Vermont.

Be temperate in wine, in eating, girls, and sloth, or the gout will seize you and plague you both. [69]

Franklin, 1734.

Better a fortune in a wife than with a wife. [22]

Mieder, TLSM, p. 51, Vermont.

Better the child's cry than the mother's sigh. [55]

Kin, p. 61.

Better the devil's than a woman's slave. [112]

Kin, p. 237.

Better to die by blows than from jealousy fade away. Better to love a dog than a thankless woman, for a dog is grateful when he is fed. [77]

Coffin and Cohen, p. 145, New Mexico.

Between a cross dog and a cross-eyed woman a house is well kept: he barks and she swings the broom. [116]

(*Variation*: A cross-grained woman and a snappish dog take good care of the house.)

Kin, p. 123.

(Hines, p. 291, Pacific Northwest.) (Danish)

Between a woman's yes and a woman's no; There's not enough room for a pin to go. [96]

[*See also:* Girls say no when they mean yes.]

[*See also:* A woman will refuse and then accept.]

Whiting, PPNC, p. 345, North Carolina. (English, German, Russian, and Spanish)

Beware of the forepart of a woman, the hind part of a mule, and all sides of a priest. [69]

(*Variation*: "every side" for "all sides")

Brunvand, Dic., p. 97.

(Brown, p. 98.)

A big wife and a big barn will never do a man any harm. [69]

Brown, p. 17.

Big woman, small feet; Small woman, all feet. [47]

Person, p. 178, #80, Washington.

Blessed is the woman who can keep a secret and the man who will not tell his wife. [88]

Mieder, Dic., p. 667, #38, Mississippi.

The blind man's wife needs no make-up. [47]

(*Variation*: "painting" for "make-up")

Kin, p. 155.

(Mieder, Dic., p. 56, #10, New York and South Carolina.) (1659) (Spanish)

(Franklin, 1736.) (German)

Borrowed wives, like borrowed books, are rarely returned. [22]
    Kin, p. 31.

Boys win girls best with flattery. [63]
    Kin, p. 282.

Bridesmaids may soon be made brides. [31]
    Kin, p. 277.

But now he is as pale and spoony as a milliner's girl. [36]
    Taylor and Whiting, p. 152, #2.

But roisterers are as quiet as lambs when they fall singly into the clutches
of a fine woman. [79]
    Taylor and Whiting, p. 213, #11.

But somehow a gal kicks over the milk pail when she lets her ebenezer
get up before a feller. [63]
    Taylor and Whiting, p. 244, milk pail.

But then you know a man can't wive and thrive the same year. [22]
    Taylor and Whiting, p. 407, wive.

Caesar's wife must be above suspicion. [22]
    Kin, p. 38.
    Titelman, p. 38.

The calmest husbands make the stormiest wives. [23]
    Brown, p. 117.
    Kin, p. 124.
    Mieder, Dic., p. 320, #14, Illinois. (1604)

A captain of industry is nothing but a buck private to his wife. [23]
    Kin, p. 39.
    Mieder, Dic., p. 82, #1, Illinois.

A career girl would rather bring home the bacon than fry it. [120]
    Brown, p. 113.

Chaste is she whom no one has asked. [100]
    Kin, p. 45.
    Mieder, Dic., p. 93, #3, Illinois. (1695)

The cheating wife doubts the chastity of all women. [100]
    Kin, p. 45.
    Mieder, Dic., p. 94, #4, Illinois.

Children, chickens, and women never have enough. [69]
    Mieder, Dic., p. 97, #11, Wisconsin.

Choose a wife on a Saturday rather than on a Sunday. [63]
    (*Variation 1*: If you want a neat wife, choose her on a Saturday.)
    (*Variation 2*: Who will have a handsome wife, let him choose her upon
a Saturday and not upon Sunday, when she is in her fine clothes.)
    [*See also*: The best time to select a wife is in the morning.]
    Kin, p. 225.

Mieder, Dic., p. 653, #14, New Jersey, New York, South Carolina. (original and 2) (1659) (Spanish)

(1. Brown, p. 139.)

(1. Franklin, 1737.)

(1. Whiting, EA, p. 482, W147.)

Choose a wife rather by your ear than your eye. [63]

[*See also*: A wife is not to be chosen by the eye only.]

Loomis, GE, p. 197, #9. (1866)

Mieder, TLSM, p. 50, Vermont.

Cold as a witch's tit. [77]

(Variation 1: Cold as a witch's titty.)

(Variation 2: Cold as a witch's tit in a brass bra.)

(Variation 3: Cold as a witch's tit at Christmas.)

(Variation 4: Cold as a witch's tit on a windy night.)

(Variation 5: Cold as the nipple on the shady side of a witch's tit.)

Clark, p. 172, #698, North Carolina.

The Colonel's lady and Judy O'Grady are sisters under the skin. [36]

(Variation: Judy O'Grady and the colonel's lady are sisters under the skin.)

Kin, p. 142.

(Whiting, PPNC, p. 350, North Carolina.)

Commend not your wife, wine nor house. [69]

Brown, p. 109.

Loomis, FA, p. 174. (1797)

Mieder, Enc., p. 526, #17377. (English)

Compliment an old hag on her lovely appearance and she'll take you at your word. [48]

Kin, p. 12.

Confound this powder—it's as slow as a woman. [36]

Taylor and Whiting, p. 409, #11.

The conversation of a woman is worth all the libraries in the world. [88]

Mieder, Dic., p. 115, #3, Wisconsin.

The cunning wife makes her husband her apron. [23]

(Variation: The cunning wife makes her husband an apron.)

Loomis, GE, p. 197, #45. (1866)

(Brown, p. 110.)

Cushions as soft as a young gal's heart. [36]

Taylor and Whiting, p. 178, #1.

Custom has given woman petticoats and man pantaloons, but it would be just as nateral for woman to wear the breeches and man the apronstring, and there is a plaguy sight of them do it too. [83]

Taylor and Whiting, p. 42, Breeches.

A dainty lady takes a pin to eat a pea. [36]

Mieder, AP, p. 90, North Carolina.

Whiting, PPNC, p. 345, North Carolina. (Jamaican)

Dally not with other folks women or money. [69]

Franklin, 1757.

Whiting, EA, p. 493, W267.

The daughter of a good mother will be the mother of a good daughter. [57]

Kin, p. 244.

The daughter of a spry old woman makes a poor housekeeper. [57]

Mieder, Dic., p. 135, #8, Mississippi.

Daughters are brittle ware. [57]

Kin, p. 64.

Mieder, Dic., p. 135, #3, Illinois. (Japanese).

Daughters-in-law become mothers-in-law. [58]

Mieder, Dic., p. 135, #2, Alaska.

Deacons' daughters and ministers' sons are the biggest devils that ever run. [57]

Mieder, Dic., p. 135, #4, Vermont. (1855)

A deaf husband and a blind wife are always a happy couple. [23]

(*Variation*: To make a happy couple, the husband must be deaf and the wife blind.)

Mieder, Dic., p. 320, #2, Illinois, Wisconsin. (1578) (also variation)

Thompson, p. 484, New York. (German)

(Kin, p. 124.)

A diamond daughter turns to glass as a wife. [57]

Mieder, Dic., p. 135, #1, New Jersey.

A dirty bread tray tells of a wasteful wife. [23]

Whiting, PPNC, p. 345, North Carolina.

Discreet wives have sometimes neither eyes nor ears. [23]

Mieder, Dic., p. 653, #15, Michigan. (1594, Shakespeare, *Romeo and Juliet*)

Don't buy a wild horse, nor marry a girl with many boyfriends. [69]

West, p. 42, Mexican-American. (1963)

Don't dare kiss an ugly girl—she'll tell the world about it. [48]

Kin, p. 263.

Don't marry a girl who wants strawberries in January. [63]

Mieder, Dic., p. 251, #7, Ohio.

Don't teach your grandmother how to milk (pick) ducks, or to suck eggs. [109]

(*Variation*: Do not try to teach your grandmother how to suck eggs.)

Atkinson, p. 79, Texas.

Bradley, p. 77, South Carolina.

(Mieder, Dic., p. 264.) (1707)

(Titelman, p. 74.)

(Whiting, MPPS, p. 267, "to teach one's grandmother to suck eggs.")
Do right and fear no man; don't write and fear no woman. **[120]**
  Mieder, Dic., p. 510, #2, Illinois, Indiana, New York. (1450)
Dull as an evening with grandma. **[109]**
  Person, p. 183, #263, Washington.
Eve was the only woman without a past. **[77]**
  Brown, p. 113.
Every child is perfect to its mother. **[55]**
  [*See also*: Every mother's child is handsome.]
  Whiting, PPNC, p. 383, North Carolina. (English)
Every girl has her day. **[120]**
  Mieder, Dic., p. 251, #8, Kentucky, Tennessee.
Every girl is beautiful in her father's eyes. **[58]**
  Mieder, Dic., p. 251, #9, Illinois.
Every Jack has his Jill; If one won't another will. **[101]**
  (*Variation 1*: There is a Jack for every Jill.)
  (*Variation 2*: There's no Jack without a Jill; if one won't, another will.)
  Mieder, Dic., p. 337, #2c.
  Thompson, p. 483, New York.
  Welsch, p. 271, Nebraska.
  (1. Adams, MCP, p. 141, #90, California.)
  (2. Mieder, TLSM, p. 55, Vermont.)
Every mother's child is handsome. **[55]**
  (*Variation 1*: Every mother thinks her child is beautiful.)
  (*Variation 2*: No mother has a homely child.)
  (*Variation 3*: There's only one pretty child in the world, and every
mother has it.)
  (*Variation 4*: A mother almost always thinks her young one handsomer
than any body else's.)
  [*See also*: Every child is perfect to its mother.]
  Kin, p. 46.
  (1. Coffin and Cohen, p. 145.)
  (1. Yoffie, p. 147, #185.) (Yiddish)
  (2. Mieder, Dic., p. 419, #5, Wisconsin.)
  (3. Whiting, PPNC, p. 383.) (German)
  (4. Whiting, PPNC, p. 383.) (American)
Everyone can keep house better than her mother, till she trieth. **[57]**
  Loomis, FA, p. 173. (1795)
Everyone can tame a shrew but him that has her. **[120]**
  (*Variation*: Every man can tame a shrew but he that hath her.)
  Kin, p. 233.
  (Loomis, GE, p. 197, #26.) (1866)
Everything goes to loose ends where there is no woman. **[36]**
  Mieder, Enc., p. 541, #17908.

Taylor and Whiting, p. 120, #9. ["ain't" for "is"]

Every wench has her sweetheart, and the dirtiest the most. **[101]**
Kin, p. 277.

Every woman is wrong until she cries, and then she is right instantly. **[36]**
Emrich, p. 67.

Every woman keeps a corner in her heart where she is always twenty-one. **[36]**
Mieder, Dic., p. 667, #39, Illinois, New York.

The exercise a woman likes most is running up bills. **[96]**
Brown, p. 113.

The eye of the housewife makes the cat fat. **[116]**
Kin, p. 123.
Mieder, Dic., p. 317, #1, Illinois.

Faint heart never won fair lady. **[63]**
(*Variation*: Faint heart never won fair lady . . . or a fat turkey.)
Adams, MCP, p. 140, #80, California.
Kin, p. 58.
Mieder, Dic., p. 292, #36. (1390)
Taylor and Whiting, p. 178, #2.
Titelman, p. 95. (1390)
Welsch, p. 271, Nebraska.
(Barbour, p. 294, Illinois.)

A fair wife without a fortune, is a fine house without furniture. **[23]**
Loomis, FA, p. 174. (1797)
Mieder, Enc., p. 525, #17344. (English)

Fair woman without virtue is like stale wine. **[77]**
Kin, p. 271.

A faithless wife is the shipwreck of a home. **[23]**
Kin, p. 6.

Far fetched and dear bought, is good for the ladies. [meaning a bargain] **[120]**
Loomis, GE, p. 197, #39. (1866)
Mieder, Dic., p. 358, #4, Michigan. (1350) ["a bargain" for "good"]

Farmers' luck: bull calves and girl babies. **[69]**
Person, p. 181, #171, Washington.

A father to his desk, a mother to her dishes. **[55]**
Kin, p. 91.
Mieder, Dic., p. 201, #14, Illinois.

Fat wives make lean husbands. **[23]**
Mieder, Dic., p. 653, #16.

Female delicacy is the best preservative of female honor. **[79]**
Hines, p. 137, Pacific Northwest.

Female is one head with two faces. **[36]**

Mieder, Dic., p. 205, #1, Florida.
The female of the species is more deadly than the male. [37]
  [from Rudyard Kipling (1865–1936) *The Female of the Species.*]
  (*Variation*: The female is the more deadly of the species.)
  Kin, p. 93.
  Mieder, Dic., p. 206, #2. (original and variation) (1911)
The female's cunning is equal to her obstinacy. [37]
  Kin, p. 93.
The fewer the women, the less the trouble. [37]
  Mieder, Dic., p. 667, #61, Illinois.
Fire dresses the meat, and not the smart lass. [120]
  Loomis, GE, p. 197, #40. (1866)
A fire scorches from near, a beautiful woman from near and from far. [48]
  Mieder, Dic., p. 209, #4, Wisconsin.
First a daughter, then a son and the family's well begun. [58]
  Mieder, Dic., p. 135, #5, New York.
The first girl up in the morning is the best-dressed girl that day. [48]
  Mieder, Dic., p. 251, #16, Illinois.
The first wife is matrimony; the second, company; the third, heresy. [23]
  Mieder, Dic., p. 654, #36. (1569) (Italian)
The first wife remembers everything. [23]
  Sparrow, p. 124.
Food and woman must go in [be appreciated] through the eyes. [48]
  West, p. 42, Mexican-American. (1962)
Fools are wise men in the affairs of women. [120]
  Loomis, GE, p. 197, #48. (1866)
  Mieder, Dic., p. 222, #65, New York.
Frailty, your name is woman. [37]
  [*See also*: Vanity, thy name is woman.]
  [*See also*: Woman thy name is curiosity.]
  Mieder, Dic., p. 232, #2, Minnesota, New York. (1600, Shakespeare) (German)
  Titelman, p. 107. (1600, Shakespeare, *Hamlet*)
French girls are virtually put on the shelf as soon as the wedding excitement is over. [23]
  Taylor and Whiting, p. 326, Shelf.
Generally speaking, woman is generally speaking. [88]
  Mieder, TLSM, p. 52, Vermont.
Generally when a man feels the need of economy he thinks it ought to begin with his wife. [23]
  Hines, p. 203, Pacific Northwest.
Gentlemen prefer blondes—but marry brunettes. [63]
  Kin, p. 28.

Getting kisses out of a woman is like getting olives out of a bottle; the first may be devilish difficult, but the rest come easy. **[101]**

(*Variation*: Kissing a girl for the first time is like getting the first olive from a jar: after the first one, they come rolling out.)

   Mieder, Dic., p. 349, #3, New York, Ohio, South Carolina.

   (Mieder, Dic., p. 251, #12, Oklahoma.)

A girl, a vineyard, an orchard, and a beanfield are hard to watch. **[101]**

   Kin, p. 275.

A girl receives—a widow takes, her husband. **[104]**

   Kin, p. 279.

A girl's first man (affair) is never forgotten. **[101]**

   (*Variation*: A woman never forgets her first love.)

   [*See also*: A young girl never quite gets over her first man.]

   Whiting, MPPS, p. 253.

   (Mieder, AP, p. 92, Pennsylvania.)

Girls learn faster than boys and forget easier. **[96]**

   Hines, p. 168, Pacific Northwest.

Girls say no when they mean yes. **[97]**

   (*Variation 1*: A woman's "no" means "yes."

   (*Variation 2*: When a lady says no, she means perhaps; when she says perhaps, she means yes; when she says yes, she is no lady.)

   (*Variation 3*: A lady says no, meaning maybe, and maybe, meaning yes; but when she says yes, she isn't a lady.)

   [*See also*: Between a woman's yes and a woman's no; There's not enough room for a pin to go.]

   [*See also*: Woman will refuse and then accept.]

   Taylor and Whiting, p. 132, #5.

   (1. Welsch, p. 271, Nebraska.)

   (2. and 3. Mieder, Dic., pp. 358–59, #11, New York, North Carolina, South Carolina.)

   (2. and 3. Titelman, p. 365.)

   (2. 1594, Shakespeare, *Two Gentlemen of Verona*)

Girls think men are all soul; women know they are all stomach. **[120]**

   Hines, p. 168, Pacific Northwest.

Girls will be girls. **[37]**

   Mieder, AP, p. 38. (American)

   Mieder, Dic., p. 251, #10. (1870–1873)

   Mieder, Enc., p. 193, #6438.

   Taylor and Whiting, p. 152, #6.

   Titelman, p. 112.

   Whiting, MPPS, p. 253.

The girl that thinks no man is good enough for her is right, but she's left. **[63]**

(*Variation in Mieder*: The girl who thinks no man is good enough for her may be right, but is now often left.)
    Mieder, Dic., p. 251, #17, Illinois, Ohio.
A girl with cotton stockings never sees a mouse. [121]
    Mieder, Dic., p. 250, #1.
A girl worth kissing is not easily kissed. [63]
    Mieder, Dic., p. 250, #2, Ohio.
Give a woman neither all your love nor all your money. [63]
    Mieder, AP, p. 65. (Mexican-American)
Give your wife the short knife, keep the long one yourself. [23]
    Hines, p. 285, Pacific Northwest. (Danish)
God could not be everywhere; therefore, He made mothers. [55]
    Kin, p. 169.
God help the man who won't marry until he finds the perfect woman, and God help him still more if he finds her. [23]
    Mieder, Dic., p. 667, #40, Illinois.
God is the guardian of a blind man's wife. [23]
    Kin, p. 93. (Hindustani)
Go down the ladder when you pick a wife; go up when you choose a friend. [64]
    Kin, p. 142.
    Mieder, Dic., p. 358, #2, Alabama, Georgia, Illinois. (1678)
Gold, women, and linen should be chosen by daylight. [69]
    Mieder, Dic., p. 257, #20, Wisconsin.
A good daughter makes a good daughter-in-law. [59]
    Yoffie, p. 149, #211. (Yiddish)
    Mieder, Enc., p. 98, #3165.
A good girl always gets caught; a bad girl knows how to avoid it. [78]
    Mieder, Dic., p. 250, #3, Kentucky, Tennessee.
The good-looking woman needs no paint. [48]
    Mieder, Dic., p. 667, #62, Illinois.
Good looks in a woman haint wuth as much to a man as good cookin' and savin' ways. [48]
    Whiting, PPNC, p. 345, North Carolina.
A good maid sometimes makes a bad wife. [23]
    Mieder, Dic., p. 395, #1, Alabama, Georgia.
A good surgeon must have an eagle's eye, a man's heart, and a lady's hand. [121]
    (*Variation*: A good surgeon must have an eagle's eye, a lady's hand, and a lion's heart.)
    Kin, p. 248.
    Mieder, Dic., p. 575, #1, Illinois, Indiana, New York. (1585)
    (Brown, p. 132.)

A good wife and health are man's best wealth. **[24]**
  Kin, p. 117.
  Franklin, 1746.
  Mieder, Enc., p. 525, #17347. (English)
  Mieder, TLSM, p. 52, Vermont. ["is a" for "are"]
  Whiting, EA, p. 482, W148. ["is" for "are"]
A good wife is a perfect lady in the living room, a good cook in the
kitchen, and a harlot in the bedroom. **[24]**
  (*Variation*: A wife should be a lady in the Parlor, a mother in the
  kitchen, and a whore in bed.)
  [*See also*: Women are saints in church, angels in the street, devils in
  the kitchen, and apes in bed.]
  Mieder, Dic., p. 653, #2, New York. (1942)
  (Whiting, MPPS, p. 682.)
A good wife is the workmanship of a good husband. **[24]**
  (*Variation*: Good wives and good plantations are made by good hus-
  bands.)
  [*See also*: A good wife makes a good husband.]
  Loomis, GE, p. 196, #6. (1866) (1736, Franklin)
  (Mieder, Dic., p. 653, #17, New York.)
A good wife lost is God's gift lost. **[24]**
  Franklin, 1733.
A good wife makes a good husband. **[24]**
  (*Contrary Variation*: A good Jack makes a good Jill.)
  Brown, p. 109. [maketh]
  Kin, p. 157.
  Loomis, FE, p. 177. (1808)
  Mieder, Dic., p. 653, #3, Indiana. (1546)
  Mieder, Enc., p. 525, #17348. (English)
  Whiting, PPNC, p. 345, North Carolina.
  (Brown, p. 116.)
Goodwill, like a good woman, is hard to get and easy to lose. **[64]**
  Mieder, Dic., p. 667, #41, New Mexico, New York.
A gracious woman retains honor. (and strong men retain riches) **[37]**
  Mieder, Dic., p. 665, #1.
The grandfathers and the grandmothers are in the children; teach them
well. **[109]**
  Zona, p. 125. (Ojibway)
Grasp at a woman and hold a nettle. **[37]**
  Whiting, EA, p. 493, W269.
Grief for a dead wife, and a troublesome guest, continues to the thresh-
old, and there is at rest. But I mean such wives as are none of the best.
[24]
  Franklin, 1734.

Mieder, Dic., p. 653, #18, New York.
A hairy man's rich, A hairy wife's a witch. [24]
   Whiting, PPNC, p. 345, North Carolina.
Handle with care women and glass. [70]
   [*See also*: Women and glass are always in danger.]
   Mieder, Dic., p. 667, #42. (1535)
The hand that rocks the cradle rules the world. [112]
   Kin, p. 59.
   Mieder, Dic., p. 276, #49. (1881)
   Whiting, MPPS, p. 282.
The happiest wife is not she that gets the best husband but she that makes
the best of that which she gets. [24]
   Mieder, Dic., p. 654, #37, New York. (1913)
Happy the bride the sun shines on. [31]
   (*Variation*: . . . and happy is the corpse that the rain pours on.)
   Hines, p. 118, Pacific Northwest. [with variations]
   Kin, p. 34.
   Mieder, Dic., p. 281, #9. (1648)
   Whiting, MPPS, p. 74.
   (Hardie, p. 463, #75.)
Having sold her skin to the devil, she bequeaths her bones to God. [78]
   Kin, p. 236.
Heaven is at the feet of mothers. [55]
   Kin, p. 117.
   Mieder, Dic., p. 295, #6, Illinois.
He gets on best with women who knows best how to get along without
them. [37]
   Brown, p. 113.
He is as gentle as a woman when he has no rival near him. [37]
   Taylor and Whiting, p. 409, #10.
He knows little who tells his wife all he knows. [24]
   Mieder, Dic., p. 653, #19, Wisconsin. (1642)
Hell hath no fury like a woman scorned. [37]
   (*Variation*: Hell knows no wrath like a woman scorned.)
   Kin, p. 118.
   Mieder, Dic., p. 296, #10, Illinois, New Jersey, Oregon. [original, with
"has" for "hath" and variation] (1696, Congreve)
   Taylor and Whiting, p. 410, #19.
   Titelman, p. 133. (Euripides; 1625, Beaumont and Fletcher, *Knight of
Malta*)
   Whiting, MPPS, p. 302. ("has" for "hath")
The hell of women is old age. [108]
   Mieder, Dic., p. 297, #15, Kentucky. (1948)
Her tongue moved like a clapper in a cowbell. [88]

Whiting, PPNC, p. 345, North Carolina.

He that has a good wife has an angel by his side; he that has a bad one has a devil at his elbow. **[24]**

Mieder, Dic., p. 653, #20, Louisiana, Michigan, New York.

He that has not got a wife is not yet a complete man. **[24]**

(*Variation*: A man without a wife is not yet a complete man.)

Mieder, Dic., p. 653, #21, New York. (1744, Franklin)

(Loomis, GE, p. 196, #7. (1755, Franklin)

He that hath a fair wife never wants trouble. **[24]**

[*See also*: He who has a fair wife needs more than two eyes.]

Hines, p. 286, Pacific Northwest.

He that hath a good wife shows it in his dress. **[24]**

Loomis, GE, p. 198, #56. (1866)

He that marries a widow will often have a dead man's head thrown into his dish. **[104]**

(*Variation*: . . . unless he has been a widower, then it is tit for tat.)

Loomis, FA, p. 175. (1802) (English and Spanish)

Mieder, Enc., p. 525, #17326. (English)

Whiting, EA, p. 482, W145. ("who" for "that," "often" before "thrown")

He that marries a widow with two daughters has three back doors to his house. [expensive] **[105]**

Whiting, PPNC, p. 345, North Carolina. (English)

Mieder, Enc., p. 525, #17322. (Scottish)

He that rides the mule shoes her. [referring to supporting a woman] **[70]**

Mieder, Dic., p. 421, #2, New York, South Carolina. (1541)

Thompson, p. 487, New York.

He that takes a wife takes care. **[25]**

Franklin, 1736.

Kin, p. 279.

Mieder, Dic., p. 653, #22, New York. (1495)

Whiting, EA, p. 482, W149.

He that tells his wife news is but newly married. **[25]**

Loomis, GE, p. 197, #41. (1866) (German)

Mieder, Dic., p. 653, #23, New Jersey. (1275)

He was as bashful as a girl. **[37]**

Taylor and Whiting, p. 152, #1.

He who has a fair wife needs more than two eyes. **[25]**

[*See also*: He that hath a fair wife never wants trouble.]

Mieder, Dic., p. 654, #24, New York. (1545)

He who has a wife has a master. **[25]**

(*Variation*: He who takes a wife finds a master.)

Brown, p. 113.

Kin, p. 158.

(Hines, p. 286, Pacific Northwest.) (French)
He who hasn't anything to do pulls his wife's eyes out. [25]
   Mieder, Dic., p. 654, #25, New York.
He who lends his wife to dance, or his horse to bullfight, has no complaint to make. [70]
   West, p. 43, Mexican-American.
He who loves his wife should watch her. [25]
   Mieder, Dic., p. 654, #26, Arkansas.
He who marries a widow with three children marries four thieves. [105]
   (*Variation*: He that marries a widow and four children marries four thieves.)
   Brown, p. 113.
   Hines, p. 285, Pacific Northwest. (Danish)
   (Mieder, Dic., p. 653, #2, New York.) (1576)
He who wishes to chastise a fool, gets him a wife. [25]
   Loomis, GE, p. 197, #42. (1866)
He who would the daughter win, with the mother must begin. [57]
   (*Variation 1*: He that would the daughter win would with the mother begin.)
   (*Variation 2*: Sweet-talk the old lady to get the daughter.)
   (*Variation 3*: Who the daughter would win with mama must begin.)
   (*Variation 4*: Salt the cow to catch the calf.)
   Kin, p. 221.
   Mieder, Dic., p. 135, #6. (1578)
   Mieder, Enc., p. 98, #3173.
   (1, 2, 3. Mieder, Dic., p. 135, #6.)
   (4. Taylor and Whiting, p. 83, #5.) (Welsh)
He would sell his grandmother for a buck. [109]
   Clark, p. 157, #298, North Carolina.
An honest woman is no better in his eyes than one of your broomstick jumpers. [78]
   Taylor and Whiting, p. 44, Broomstick.
The honest woman should never believe herself alone. [79]
   West, p. 42, Mexican-American. (1963)
Hotter than a grass widow's kiss. [a grass widow is a divorcée.] [105]
   Taylor, PCSC, p. 50.
House goes mad when women gad. [116]
   Mieder, Dic., pp. 315–316, #20, Kansas, Wisconsin. (1822)
A house well-furnished makes a good housewife. [116]
   Kin, p. 123.
A house without a woman and firelight, is like a body without soul or sprite. [117]
   Franklin, 1733.
   Mieder, AP, p. 39. ("women" for "a woman") (American)

Mieder, Dic., p. 315, #6, New York, South Carolina.

A house without a woman is like a boat without a rudder. **[117]**

Mieder, AP, p. 59. (Italian)

How many times, while sighing, is a woman laughing. **[37]**

West, p. 42, Mexican-American.

Husband and wife are one flesh. **[25]**

Coffin and Cohen, p. 145.

Yoffie, p. 149, #206. (Yiddish)

The husband is the head of the house, but the wife is the neck—and the neck moves the head. **[112]**

(*Variation*: Man is the head, but woman turns it.)

Mieder, Dic., p. 320, #15, North Carolina.

(Kin, p. 282.)

I couldn't . . . no more than I would strike my granny. **[109]**

Taylor and Whiting, p. 158, #3.

I'de as leaf travel as stay home with a scoldin' wife, cryin' children, and a smoky chimney. **[70]**

Taylor and Whiting, p. 402, #1.

If a man is unfaithful to his wife, it's like spitting from a house into the street; but if a woman is unfaithful to her husband, it's like spitting from the street into the house. **[25]**

Kin, p. 265.

If a woman drowns, hunt her upstream. **[121]**

Hines, p. 291, Pacific Northwest.

If one woman were to tell the truth about her life, the whole world would split open. **[121]**

Mason, 3B.

If the gal means to git married, her bread will be all dough agin. **[64]**

Taylor and Whiting, p. 41, Bread.

If the girls won't run after the men, the men will run after them. **[64]**

Mieder, AP, p. 38. (American)

Mieder, Enc., p. 193, #6441.

Taylor and Whiting, p. 152, #9.

If the newly-married couple were to dance together on their wedding day, the wife would thenceforth rule the roast. [roost] **[25]**

Taylor and Whiting, p. 308, Roast.

If there were not bad women, there would be no bad men. **[78]**

Whiting, EA, p. 293, W271. (1774)

If the wife sins, the husband is equally guilty. **[25]**

Kin, p. 6.

If you can kiss the mistress never kiss the maid. **[101]**

(*Variation*: Never kiss the maid if you can kiss the mistress.)

Kin, p. 140.

Mieder, Dic., p. 414, Texas, Wisconsin. (1659)

(Whiting, EA, p. 274, M9.)

If you don't obey your mother, you will obey your stepmother. **[55]**
  Mieder, Dic., p. 419, #3, Wisconsin.

If you make your wife an ass, she will make you an ox. **[25]**
  Kin, p. 216. [under retaliation]

If you marry a beautiful blonde, you marry trouble. **[25]**
  Kin, p. 157.
  Mieder, Dic., p. 407, #2, Illinois. (1936)

If your wife is small, bend down to take her counsel. **[25]**
  Mieder, Dic., p. 654, #27, New York. (1948)

If you take a wife from hell, she will bring you back. **[25]**
  Mieder, Enc., p. 527, #17407.
  Whiting, EA, p. 482, W150. (1793)

If you take the child by the hand, you take the mother by the heart. **[55]**
  Kin, p. 169.

If you want to know a bad husband, look at his wife's countenance. **[25]**
  Hines, p. 181, Pacific Northwest.

I have an idea that gall will either die a sour old maid, or have to take a crooked stick for a husband at last. **[94]**
  Taylor and Whiting, p. 354, #8.

An ill-tempered woman is the devil's door-mail. **[78]**
  Hines, p. 291, Pacific Northwest. (Danish)

I'm as tender as a mother to you. **[55]**
  Taylor and Whiting, p. 251, #1.

The impatient virgin becomes a mother without being a bride. **[101]**
  Kin, p. 128.

Inconstant as a woman's love. **[97]**
  Whiting, EA, p. 494, W286. (1803)

In craft women can give points to the devil. **[78]**
  Hines, p. 294, Pacific Northwest.

Is a woman ever satisfied? No, if she were she wouldn't be a woman. **[37]**
  Mieder, Dic., p. 667, #43, New Jersey.

It is a fool who loves a woman from afar. **[64]**
  Mieder, Dic., p. 224, #117, Indiana.

It is a good man that never stumbles, and a good wife than never grumbles. **[25]**
  (*Variation*: "horse" for "man") (Spanish)
  Kin, p. 245. (original and variation)

It is as easy to love a rich girl as a poor one. **[64]**
  Mieder, Dic., p. 251, #11, New Jersey, New York. (1941)

It is a thing that's indisputable; Women, like winds, are very mutable. **[97]**
  Whiting, EA, p. 494, W286. (1748)

It is a woman's privilege to change her mind. **[97]**

(*Variation 1*: Every woman has the divine privilege of changing her mind.)

(*Variation 2*: Ladies have leave to change their minds.)

(*Variation 3*: To change the mind is a lady's privilege.)

(*Variation 4*: A woman may change her mind.)

Mieder, Dic., p. 667, #44, Michigan, New York, South Carolina. (1616)

(1 and 2. Kin, p. 282.)

(3. Mieder, Dic., p. 358, #10, New York, South Carolina.) (English) (1500)

(4. Whiting, MPPS, p. 694.)

It is better to dwell in the corner of a housetop than with a brawling woman in a wide house. **[117]**

(*Variation*: It's better to live on the top of the house than with a contentious woman.)

Mieder, Dic., p. 667, #45, Alabama, Georgia. (1948)

(Mieder, TLSM, p. 51, Vermont.)

It is cheaper to find a wife than to feed a wife. **[26]**

Kin, p. 279.

Mieder, Dic., p. 654, #28, Illinois.

It is easier to find a white crow than a good woman. **[78]**

West, p. 43, Mexican-American. (1963)

It is given to women alone to be in love and still retain their self-respect. **[64]**

Brown, p. 114.

It is harder to marry a daughter well than to bring her up well. **[58]**

Mieder, Dic., p. 135, #7, North Dakota. (1732)

It is hard to be a biddy and a lady too. **[37]**

Mieder, Dic., p. 50, New York, South Carolina.

It is ill with the roost when the hens crow and the cock must remain silent. **[84]**

Smith and Eddins, p. 240, Texas.

It is not the nature of the female tongue to be silent. **[88]**

Whiting, EA, p. 494, W280. (1792)

It is said that when a woman wets her finger fleas had better flee. **[112]**

Taylor and Whiting, p. 133, #10.

It never occurs to a fashionable woman that there is enough goods in the train of her dress to make a poor child a Sunday frock. **[97]**

Hines, p. 291, Pacific Northwest.

It's a poor bride who cannot help some. **[31]**

Mieder, Dic., p. 70, #5, Vermont.

It's a poor house that can't afford one lady. **[37]**

Mieder, Dic., p. 316, #24, Kansas, New York.

Thompson, p. 487, New York. ["support" for "afford"]
It's a poor family that has neither a whore nor a thief in it. [93]
   Kin, p. 195. [under poverty]
   Mieder, Dic., p. 474, #15, New York, South Carolina. (1566)
It's a sweet sorrow to bury a nagging wife. [26]
   Kin, p. 35.
It's a wise child that knows his own mother in a bathing suit. [extremes
of fashion] [55]
   Whiting, PPNC, p. 345, North Carolina. (English)
It's a woman's maxim, "False in a small degree, false in every degree."
[121]
   Brunvand, Dic., p. 46.
It's enough to make a Quaker kick his grandmother. [109]
   Taylor and Whiting, p. 300, #2.
It's like the old woman's soap—if it don't go ahead, it goes back. [108]
   Taylor and Whiting, p. 409, #18.
It takes a mother to be so blind she can't tell black from white. [55]
   Mieder, AP, p. 81, Colorado.
It takes a smart woman to be a fool. [37]
   Mieder, Dic., p. 667, #46, Maryland.
It takes as much wit not to displease a woman as it takes little to please
her. [37]
   Hines, p. 289, Pacific Northwest.
It takes a wise woman to be an old maid. [94]
   Mieder, Dic., p. 667, #47, New York.
It takes two old women to make a cheese: one to hold and the other to
squeeze. [108]
   Mieder, Dic., p. 667, #48, Maine.
I would have a woman as true as Death. [121]
   Taylor and Whiting, p. 95, #20.
A jealous woman is worse than a witch. [78]
   Kin, p. 135.
John Do-little was the son of good-wife Spin-little. [56]
   Loomis, FA, p. 177. (1808)
Judge a maiden at the kneading pan, not at the dance. [64]
   Hines, p. 197, Pacific Northwest. (Danish)
June brides, January mothers. [56]
   Mieder, Dic., p. 70, #6, New York.
Keep a mistress seven years and you'll find her as useful as a wife. [101]
   Kin, p. 282.
Keep the ladies busy and that keeps them out of mischief. [84]
   Mieder, Dic., p. 358, #5, New York, South Carolina. (1908)
A kind wife makes a faithful husband. [26]

Mieder, Dic., p. 653, #4, Michigan.
Kissing a girl because she is willing is like scratching a place that doesn't itch. **[64]**
Mieder, TLSM, p. 51, Vermont.
Ladies don't smoke. **[84]**
Mieder, Dic., p. 358, #6, North Carolina.
Ladies first. **[84]**
Whiting, MPPS, p. 357.
Ladies in slacks should not turn their backs. **[84]**
Mieder, Dic., p. 358, #7, Oregon.
Ladies will sooner pardon want of sense than want of manners. **[112]**
Loomis, GE, p. 197, #35. (1866)
Ladies young and fair have the gift to know it. **[48]**
Mieder, Dic., p. 358, #8, Kansas, New York, South Carolina. (1599, Shakespeare)
A lady is a woman who makes it easy for a man to be a gentleman. **[121]**
Mieder, Dic., p. 358, #1, Illinois.
A lady is known by the product she endorses. **[38]**
Mieder, Dic., p. 358, #2, New York, South Carolina. (1936)
A lass that has many wooers oft fares the worst. **[64]**
Loomis, GE, p. 197, #21. (1866)
The last generation will be female. **[121]**
Sparrow, p. 125.
The last suitor wins the maid. **[64]**
Kin, p. 137. [under judgment]
Mieder, Dic., p. 572. (1611) (English, French) (1611)
A lazy girl and a warm bed are hard to separate. **[78]**
Kin, p. 145.
A lazy wife and a large barn bring luck to any man. **[70]**
Mieder, Dic., p. 653, #5, New York.
Left to dance in a hog trough. [said of a girl who has been jilted or of an older sister whose younger one has married before her] **[94]**
Hardie, p. 470, #127.
Let not the maid become the mistress. **[84]**
Whiting, EA, p. 273, M7.
Let the women wear the breeches. **[112]**
Mieder, Dic., p. 667, #49, Mississippi. (1564)
Let thy maid-servant be faithful, strong and homely. **[48]**
Franklin, 1736.
The level of the woman is the level of the world. **[79]**
Mieder, Dic., p. 667, #63, North Carolina.
Light-heel'd mothers make leaden-heeled daughters. **[57]**
Franklin, 1745.
Whiting, EA, p. 297, M257.

A light wife makes a heavy husband. **[26]**
  Mieder, Dic., p. 653, #6, New York. (1597, Shakespeare)
Like a gal's mind, no two minits alike. **[97]**
  Taylor and Whiting, p. 245, #1.
Like mother, like daughter. **[57]**
  (*Variation*: As is the mother, so is the daughter.)
  Mieder, Dic., p. 419, #2. (original and variation) (1300)
  Titelman, p. 218. (1300) (American, 1644)
  Whiting, EA, p. 297, M258. (1644)
  Whiting, PPNC, p. 346, North Carolina. (English)
A little bit of powder and a little bit of paint makes a woman look like what she ain't. **[48]**
  (*Variation 1*: . . . makes an ugly woman . . .)
  (*Variation 2*: . . . can make you look like what you ain't.)
  (*Variation 3*: Powder and paint make a girl look what she ain't.)
  Mieder, Dic., p. 478, #1. (original and all variations)
Little girls have little wit. **[38]**
  Mieder, AP, p. 38. (American)
  Mieder, Enc., p. 194, #6444.
  Taylor and Whiting, p. 152, #7.
Little girls shouldn't ask questions. **[84]**
  Taylor and Whiting, p. 152, #8.
A little house well filled, a little land well tilled, and a little wife well willed are great riches. **[70]**
  Kin, p. 219.
  Franklin, 1735. ["field" for "land"]
  Loomis, GE, p. 196, #3.
  Mieder, Dic., p. 315, #7, Mississippi, New York, South Carolina.
The longest five years in a woman's life is between twenty-nine and thirty. **[48]**
  Mieder, Dic., pp. 667–68, #64.
Long thread, lazy girl. **[38]**
  Person, p. 179, #91, Washington.
Look after your wife; never mind yourself, she'll look after you. **[26]**
  Hines, p. 286, Pacific Northwest.
Lots of men get women, but few get wives. **[26]**
  Mieder, Dic., p. 654, #29, Kentucky, Tennessee.
A maid that laughs is half taken. **[64]**
  Whiting, MPPS, p. 392.
Maids are drawn to pleasure as moths to the flame. **[38]**
  Kin, p. 192.
Maids want nothing but husbands, and then they want everything. **[38]**
  Loomis, FA, p. 174. (1797)
  Mieder, Dic., p. 395, #2. (1678) (English)

Manage the horse with the reins, the woman with the spur. **[70]**
West, p. 43, Mexican-American. (1963)
A man cannot possess anything better than a good woman, nor anything
worse than a bad one. **[70]**
Hines, p. 197, Pacific Northwest.
A man can't serve two mistresses—his country and his wife. **[26]**
Taylor and Whiting, p. 247, #1.
A man chases a woman until she catches him. **[64]**
Kin, p. 282.
Mieder, Dic., p. 396, #12, California, New York. [Also, "girl" for
"woman"]
A man doesn't want a woman smarter than he is. **[84]**
Mieder, Dic., p. 396, #15, North Carolina.
A man earns and the woman spends. **[97]**
Mieder, AP, p. 61. (Italian)
Man gets and forgets, woman gives and forgives. **[38]**
Thompson, p. 483, New York.
Mieder, Dic., p. 400, #125, New York, South Carolina.
The man had three or four daughters who, as the phrase goes "gave you
a good deal for your money." [i.e., were entertaining] **[58]**
Taylor and Whiting, p. 248, #9.
A man must ask his wife's leave to thrive. **[26]**
(*Variation 1*: A man must ask his wife to thrive.)
(*Variation 2*: A man must ask his wife if he may be rich.)
Loomis, FA, p. 174. (1797)
(1. Loomis, GE, p. 197, #38.) (1866)
(2. Hines, p. 198, Pacific Northwest.)
A man of straw is worth a woman of gold. **[38]**
Brown, p. 110.
Loomis, GE, p. 197, #50. (1866) (French)
A man's best fortune, or his worst, is his wife. **[26]**
(*Variation*: "virtue" for "fortune"
Loomis, FA, p. 173. (1795)
Loomis, GE, p. 197, #23. ("a wife" for "his wife") (1866)
(Brown, p. 109.) (Spanish)
A man-servant knows more than he tells; a maid-servant tells more than
she knows. **[88]**
Kin, p. 156.
A man that cheats his wife may cheat many others. **[26]**
Mieder, TLSM, p. 55, Vermont.
A man thinks he knows, but a woman knows better. **[38]**
Mieder, Dic., p. 397, #39. (1938)
A man who is wise is only as wise as his wife thinks he is. **[26]**

Mieder, Dic., p. 397, #41, New York, South Carolina.
A man who kicks his dog will beat his wife. [26]
   Mieder, AP, p. 85, Kentucky.
The man who never praises his wife deserves to have a poor one. [26]
   Hines, p. 200, Pacific Northwest.
A man without ambition is like a woman without looks. [48]
   Mieder, Dic., p. 16, #1, New York. (1900)
A man without a wife is like a fork without a knife. [26]
   Loomis, GE, p. 196, #7. (1866)
Man works from sun to sun, But woman's work is never done. [84]
   (*Variation 1*: A woman's work is never done.)
   (*Variation 2*: A woman's work is never at an end.)
   (*Variation 3*: A man works from dawn to setting sun, but a woman's work is never done.)
   (*Variation 4*: Man's work lasts till set of sun; woman's work is never done.)
   Mieder, Dic., p. 401, #150. [a woman's] (1570)
   Thompson, p. 487, New York.
   Whiting, PPNC, p. 346, North Carolina.
   (1. Kin, p. 284.)
   (1. Whiting, EA, p. 494, W283.) (1722)
   (1. and 4. Mieder, Dic., p. 666, #31.) (1570)
   (2. and 3. Loomis, GE, p. 197, #33.) (1866)
Many a man sees a wolf at the door because his wife sees a mink in the window. [26]
   Mieder, Dic., p. 665, #10, Mississippi.
Many blame the wife for their own thriftless life. [26]
   Loomis, GE, p. 197, #52. (1866)
Many estates are spent in getting/ Since women for tea forsook spinning and knitting/ And men, for Punch, forsook hewing and splitting. [78]
   Franklin, 1733.
   Mieder, Dic., p. 183, #2. [1st line only]
Marriage is the supreme blunder that all women make. [26]
   Brown, p. 114.
Marry your daughter and eat fresh fish betimes. [58]
   Franklin, 1736.
   Whiting, EA, p. 94, D20. (English)
Marry your son when you will, your daughter when you can. [58]
   (*Variation*: Marry your son when you please, and your daughter when you can.)
   Franklin, 1734.
   Thompson, p. 483, New York. (plural)
   Mieder, TLSM, p. 56, Vermont. (plural)

(Mieder, Dic., p. 552, #9, Indiana, New York.) (1640)

Matrimony is an insane idea on the part of a man to pay some woman's board. [27]

(*Variation*: Matrimony has been defined to be an insane idea on the part of a man to pay some woman's board.)

Emrich, p. 67.

(Hendricks, p. 92, Texas.)

Mean enough to steal the pennies from his Grandmother's eyes. [109]

Hardie, p. 470, #138.

Measure that woman . . . for a pair of breeches; she's detarmined to wear 'em. [84]

Taylor and Whiting, p. 42, Breeches.

The men and dogs for the barn, the women and cats for the kitchen. ["There is an appropriate place for everything."] [84]

Adams, TPSFC, p. 62, #75, California.

Men aren't worth the salt of a woman's tears. [38]

Mieder, TLSM, p. 53, Vermont.

Men are virtuous because the women are; women are virtuous from necessity. [79]

Brunvand, Dic., p. 92.

Men build houses; women build homes. [84]

Mieder, Dic., p. 402, #163. (1938)

Men gossip as much as women do, but not so meanly. [89]

Hines, p. 210, Pacific Northwest.

Men love women; women love men. [64]

Hines, p. 210, Pacific Northwest.

Men never learn anything about women, but they have a lot of fun trying. [121]

Brown, p. 113.

Men seldom make passes at girls who wear glasses. [64]

Kin, p. 106.

Mieder, Dic., p. 251, #13. (1926)

Men's fortunes and women's hearts stand a great deal of breaking. [121]

Taylor and Whiting, p. 409, #8.

Men's hearts are full of deceit, and women are their confiding victims. [121]

Loomis, GE, p. 198, #84. (1866)

Men should be careful lest they cause women to weep, for God counts their tears. [38]

Hines, p. 210, Pacific Northwest.

The Mistress makes the morning, But the Lord makes the afternoon. [38]

Taylor and Whiting, p. 247, #3.

Modesty becomes a virgin, but it's a vice in a widow. [105]

Kin, p. 166.

Modesty is a quality in a lover more praised by the woman than liked.
[101]
    Kin, p. 167.
    Mieder, Dic., p. 414, #2, Illinois.
The more a girl runs, the harder a boy chases. **[64]**
    Mieder, Dic., p. 251, #18, Kansas.
More commotion than a whorehouse on Saturday night. **[93]**
    Taylor, PCSC, p. 29.
The more men love their glasses, the less they love their wives. **[27]**
    Loomis, GE, p. 197, #51. (1866)
The more women look in their glass the less they look in their house.
[117]
    [akin to: "The more a woman admires her face, the more she ruins
her house." (Spanish)]
    (*Variation 1*: The more women look in their glasses, the less they look
to their houses.)
    (*Variation 2*: "heart" for "house")
    [*See also*: The wife who loves the looking-glass hates the saucepan.]
Kin, p. 268.
    (1. Loomis, GE, p. 197.) (1866) (English)
    (2. Loomis, FA, p. 173.) (1796)
The morning rain is like an old woman's dance, soon over. **[108]**
    (*Variation*: A morning's rain is like an old woman's dance: it doesn't
last long.)
    Boatwright, p. 219, Texas, North Carolina. (English, German)
    Smith and Eddins, p. 244, Texas.
    (Mieder, Dic., p. 498, #2, Mississippi, South Carolina.) (1640)
The most dreadful thing against women is the character of the men that
praise them. **[48]**
    Hines, p. 294, Pacific Northwest.
The most fascinating women never make the best marriages. **[27]**
    Brown, p. 114.
Most men get as good a wife as they deserve. **[27]**
    Mieder, Dic., p. 654, #30, New York. (1948)
Most women are better out of their houses than in them. **[117]**
    Hines, p. 294, Pacific Northwest.
A mother can take care of ten children, but sometimes ten children can't
take care of one mother. **[56]**
    Titelman, p. 239. (Jewish)
Mother-in-law and daughter-in-law are a tempest and a hailstorm. **[56]**
    Whiting, EA, p. 298, M263.
The mother-in-law is a queer invention, as full of flaws and dangers as a
second-hand steam boiler. **[56]**
    Taylor and Whiting, p. 351, Steam boiler.

The mother-in-law remembers not that she was a daughter-in-law. **[56]**
   (*Variation*: No mother-in-law ever remembers that she was once a daughter-in-law.)
   Mieder, Dic., p. 419, Minnesota, North Carolina. (1594)
   (Brown, p. 115.)
Mother knows best. **[56]**
   (*Variation*: Mother knows best; father pays less.)
   Kin, p. 169.
   Mieder, Dic., p. 419, #4. (1958)
   Whiting, MPPS, p. 427.
   (Mieder, Dic., p. 419, #4.) (1927)
The mother knows best whether the child is like the father. **[56]**
   Kin, p. 186. [under paternity]
Motherless husband makes happy wife. **[27]**
   (*Variation*: She's the happiest wife that marries the son of a dead mother.)
   Mieder, Dic., p. 320, #11.
   (Brown, p. 115.)
Mother's darlings make but milk-porridge heroes. **[56]**
   Loomis, FA, p. 175. (1798)
Mother's love is best of all. **[56]**
   Mieder, Dic., p. 389, #86, Wisconsin. (1814)
A mother's love will dash up from the depths of the sea. **[56]**
   Kin, p. 169.
A mother's tears are the same in all languages. **[56]**
   Hines, p. 216, Pacific Northwest.
A mother wants her daughter married well, but her sister doesn't want her married better than she is. **[57]**
   Mieder, Dic., p. 419, #1, California.
A mule that whinnies and a woman that talks Latin never come to any good. **[84]**
   Brunvand, Dic., p. 97.
Music is the key to the female heart. **[38]**
   Kin, p. 171.
   Mieder, Dic., p. 421, #2, Illinois.
My farm troubles me, for a farm and a wife soon run wild if left alone long. **[70]**
   Taylor and Whiting, p. 127, farm.
My son is my son till he gets him a wife; but my daughter's my daughter all the days of her life. **[58]**
   (*Variation*: A daughter is a daughter all the days of her life, but a son is a son till he gets him a wife.)
   Kin, p. 46.
   Mieder, Dic., p. 552, #4. ["a" for "my"] (1670) (English)

(Whiting, MPPS, p. 150.)
Nature makes women to be won, and men to win. **[84]**
  (*Variation*: Nature framed all women to be won.)
  Kin, p. 172.
  Mieder, Dic., p. 424, #13, Illinois.
  (Kin, p. 287.)
Nature meant woman to be her masterpiece. **[38]**
  Kin, p. 281.
A neat maiden often makes a dirty wife. **[27]**
  Mieder, Dic., p. 395, #2.
Need makes the old wife trot. [akin to "Money makes the mare go."]
[108]
  Loomis, FA, p. 177. (1821) (English)
  Mieder, Dic., p. 426, #2, Oklahoma, Texas. (1225)
Ne'er seek a wife till you know what to do with her. **[27]**
  Mieder, Dic., p. 654, #31.
Ne'er take a wife till thou hast a house (and a fire) to put her in. **[27]**
  Franklin, 1733.
  Whiting, EA, p. 482, W151.
Neither a fortress nor a maid will hold out long after they begin to parley.
[101]
  Brown, p. 140, from Franklin.
Never marry a widow unless her first husband was hanged. **[105]**
  Brown, p. 100. (Celtic)
  Mieder, Dic., p. 653, #3, Wisconsin. (1721) (Scottish)
Never pick women or horses by candlelight. **[70]**
  Kin, p. 39.
Never praise your wife until you have been married ten years. **[27]**
  Mieder, Dic., p. 654, #32, Arkansas.
Never quarrel with a woman. **[38]**
  Mieder, Dic., p. 667, #51, Indiana. (1875) (Chinese)
Never run after a woman or a streetcar: there'll be another along in a
few minutes. **[70]**
  (*Variation*: Never run after a woman. They are like streetcars. Stand
still, for another one will come along soon.)
  Mieder, Dic., p. 667, #52, Michigan, New York, Pennsylvania.
  (Mieder, TLSM, p. 50, Vermont.)
Never trust a red-headed woman. **[121]**
  Person, p. 178, #75, Washington.
Next to no wife, a good wife is best. **[27]**
  Loomis, GE, p. 197, #12. (1866)
  Mieder, Dic., p. 654, #33, New Jersey. (1497)
A nice wife and a back door oft do make a rich man poor. **[27]**
  Mieder, Dic., p. 653, #7, New York. (1450) (English)

A no-account wife takes advice from everyone but her husband. **[27]**
  Mieder, Dic., p. 653, #8, Mississippi.
No argument can convince a woman or a stubborn ass. **[38]**
  Kin, p. 14.
  Mieder, Dic., p. 26, #7, Illinois, North Carolina. ["will" for "can"]
The noblest sight on earth is a man talking reason and his wife listening
to him. **[84]**
  Hendricks, p. 92, Texas.
No fish without bones; no woman without a temper. **[38]**
  Kin, p. 253.
No house is big enough for two women. **[117]**
  (*Variation 1*: "was ever" for "is")
  (*Variation 2*: No home large enough for two women to manage.)
  (*Variation 3*: Two women cannot live under one roof.)
  [*See also*: Two women in the same house can never agree.]
  Adams, TPSFC, p. 62, #63, California.
  Whiting, MPPS, p. 693. (Oriental)
  (1 and 2. Mieder, Dic., p. 316, #28, Maryland, Mississippi. (1450)
  (3. Mieder, Dic., p. 668, #76.)
  Adams, TPSFC, p. 62, #63, California.
  Mieder, Dic., p. 316, #28, Maryland, Mississippi. ["was ever" for "is"]
(original and variation 1) (1450)
  Whiting, MPPS, p. 693. (Oriental)
  (Mieder, Dic., p. 668, #76.)
No Indian ever sold his daughter for a name. **[58]**
  "Indian Proverbs," p. 173.
  Mieder, AP, p. 106, Oklahoma.
No man is a hero to his wife or his butler. **[27]**
  Kin, p. 119.
  Mieder, Dic., p. 299, #5c. (1603)
No padlocks, bolts or bars can secure a maiden as well as her own re-
serve. **[79]**
  Kin, p. 215.
No prison is fair, no mistress foul. **[101]**
  (*Variation*: There are no ugly loves nor handsome prisons.)
  Kin, p. 166.
  (Mieder, Dic., p. 390, #99, Illinois.)
Nothing dries sooner than a woman's tears. **[38]**
  Loomis, FA, p. 174. (1798)
  Mieder, Dic., p. 584, #4, Oklahoma, Texas. (1563)
Nothing on arth puts a feller to his stump like pulling in the same team
with a purty gal. **[27]**
  Taylor and Whiting, p. 359, #5.

Nothing will ruin an interesting intellectual conversation any quicker than the arrival of a pretty girl. [121]
  Mieder, Dic., p. 251, #14, New York.
No woman is too silly not to have a genius for spite. [78]
  Hines, p. 291, Pacific Northwest.
No woman is ugly if she is well dressed. [49]
  (*Variation*: No woman is ugly when she is dressed.)
  Kin, p. 263. (Portuguese, Spanish)
  (Loomis, GE, p. 197, #43.) (1866)
No woman likes to hear her male friends ridiculed. [121]
  Hines, p. 292, Pacific Northwest.
No woman should ever be quite accurate about her age: it looks so calculating. [49]
  Mieder, Dic., p. 667, #53, New York.
No women indulged like the American. [121]
  Whiting, EA, p. 493, W272. (1774)
A nurse spoils a good housewife. [117]
  Kin, p. 177.
  Mieder, Dic., p. 434, #1, Illinois. (1659) (English)
An obedient wife commands her husband. [27]
  (*Variation 1*: The woman who obeys her husband rules him.)
  (*Variation 2*: A virtuous woman commands her husband by obeying him.)
  Mieder, Enc., p. 526, #17373. (English)
  Loomis, GE, p. 196, #5. (1866)
  (1. Mieder, Dic., p. 320, #18, Utah.) (1642)
  (2. Kin, p. 271.)
  (2. Mieder, Dic., p. 634, #1, Illinois.) (Syrus)
Observe the mother and take the daughter. [57]
  Mieder, Dic., p. 419, #6, Wisconsin.
Of all the paths leading to a woman's love, pity is the straightest. [64]
  Hines, p. 225, Pacific Northwest.
Oh a woman is always a woman. [38]
  Brunvand, Dic., p. 154.
An old bachelor is fussy because he has never had a wife to fuss at him. [28]
  Mieder, Dic., p. 33, #8, North Carolina.
The old cat refuses to admit that the face in the looking glass is her own. [49]
  Kin, p. 151.
Old houses and old ladies always need repairing. [108]
  [*See also*: A ship and a woman are ever repairing.]
  Kin, p. 214.

The old ladies always interfere and make you walk right straight up to the chalk, whether or no. **[109]**

Taylor and Whiting, p. 64, #14.

An old maid doesn't know anything but what she imagines. **[94]**

[*See also*: What a woman does not know she imagines.]

Mieder, TLSM, p. 50, Vermont.

Old maids fancy nobody knows how to bring up children but them. **[94]**

Mieder, Dic., p. 395, #3, Nebraska, New York, North Carolina, South Carolina. (1546) (English)

Taylor and Whiting, p. 233, #3.

Old maids lead apes in hell. **[94]**

(*Variation*: Old maids lead apes there, where the old batchelors are turn'd to apes.)

(Franklin, 1735.)

Whiting, EA, p. 274, M10.

Whiting, MPPS, p. 392.

Old maids make good lovers. (An old hen makes a good stew.) **[101]**

West, p. 43, Mexican-American.

An old man marrying a young girl is like buying a book for someone else to read. **[101]**

Thompson, p. 484, New York.

Mieder, TLSM, p. 56, Vermont.

Old wives and children [originally "bairns"] make fools of physicians. **[109]**

Brown, p. 129.

Mieder, Dic., p. 654, #34, New York. (1721) (Scottish)

The old woman is picking her geese. [old woman = Mother Nature; It is snowing] **[109]**

Whiting, PPNC, p. 499, North Carolina. (English)

Old woman's gold is not ugly. **[109]**

(*Variation*: An old female's gold is never ugly.)

Mieder, Dic., p. 257, #26, Wisconsin. (1732)

(Kin, p. 93)

The old woman would not have sought her daughter in the oven if she had not been there herself. **[57]**

Whiting, EA, p. 493, W273.

Once a lady, always a lady. **[38]**

Mieder, Dic., p. 358, #9, New York, South Carolina.

Once a whore, always a whore. **[93]**

Kin, p. 279.

Mieder, Dic., p. 652, #1, Illinois. (1613)

Mieder, Enc., p. 524, #17306. (English)

Once a woman has given you her heart you can never get rid of the rest of her. **[38]**

Kin, p. 281.

Mieder, Dic., p. 667, #54, Illinois. (1696)

One girl is a girl, two girls are half a girl, and three girls are no girl at all. [39]

Mieder, Dic., p. 251, #15, Kentucky, Tennessee. (1930)

One good husband is worth two good wives; for the scarcer things are the more they're valued. [28]

Kin, p. 124.

One hair of a woman draws more than a team of horses. [64]

Brown, p. 35. (sixteenth century)

Mieder, Dic., p. 667, #55. (1591)

One sorrow drowns another; yesterday my husband died, and today I lost my needle. [105]

Thompson, p. 490, New York.

One tongue is enough for two women. [89]

Mieder, Dic., p. 604, #25. (1732)

Onions can make ev'n heirs and widows weep. [105]

Franklin, 1734.

Kin, p. 180.

Mieder, AP, p. 88, New York.

Thompson, p. 484, New York.

The only difficulty in being able to read women like a book is that you are liable to forget your place. [121]

Brown, p. 113.

Only nice girls blush. [79]

Person, p. 179, #88, Washington.

The only secret a woman can keep is that of her age. [89]

Kin, p. 227.

Mieder, Dic., p. 529, #16, Kentucky, Tennessee. (1732)

The only way to get the upper hand of a woman is not to be more woman than she is herself. [39]

Hines, p. 292, Pacific Northwest.

An opinion formed by a woman is inflexible; the fact is not so stubborn. [39]

Hines, p. 222, Pacific Northwest. [Hines associates with "Women will have their wills."]

Our girlhood determines our womanhood. [39]

Mieder, Dic., p. 251, Florida.

Plain women are as safe as churches. [49]

Kin, p. 282.

Mieder, Dic., p. 667, #56, Illinois.

Play, women and wine undo men laughing. [70]

Loomis, FA, p. 173. (1795) (English, 1670)

A poor beauty is in double jeopardy: her beauty tempts others, her poverty, herself. **[49]**
    Kin, p. 135.
The premonitory symptoms of love are as evident to women as are those of any other eruptive disease about to break out to a Philadelphia doctor. **[39]**
    Taylor and Whiting, p. 282, Philadelphia Doctor.
The proof of gold is fire; the proof of woman, gold; the proof of man, a woman. **[121]**
    (*Variation*: Gold is tested by fire, men by gold.)
    Kin, p. 254.
    Franklin, 1733.
    (Mieder, Dic., p. 256, #11.) (1666) (Italian)
    (Mieder, TLSM, p. 51, Vermont.)
Prouder than an old maid with a new feller. **[94]**
    Taylor, PCSC, p. 64.
A proud woman brings distress on her family. **[85]**
    Kin, p. 202.
    Mieder, Dic., p. 488, #2, Illinois. (Cingalese)
A quiet wife is mighty pretty. **[28]**
    Kin, p. 279.
    Mieder, Dic., p. 653, #9, Illinois.
Rather spoil your joke than roil your wife. **[28]**
    Kin, p. 135.
A rich bride goes young to the church. **[31]**
    Mieder, Dic., p. 70, #1, Wisconsin.
A rich man is never ugly in the eyes of a girl. **[65]**
    Kin, p. 218.
    Mieder, Dic., p. 508, #7, Illinois.
The rich widow cries with one eye and rejoices with the other. **[105]**
    (*Variation*: A rich widow weeps with one eye and laughs with the other.)
    Brown, p. 112. (cries, laughs)
    Loomis, GE, p. 197, #29. (1866)
    West, p. 42, Mexican-American. (cries, smiles)
    (Mieder, Enc., p. 524, #17319.) (Portuguese)
Rich widows are the only second-hand goods that sell at prime cost. **[105]**
    Hendricks, p. 92, Texas. [attributed to Franklin]
Rooster, horse, and woman should be chosen by breed. **[70]**
    West, p. 43, Mexican-American. (1963)
Rule a wife and have a wife. **[28]**
    Mieder, Dic., p. 654, #35, Kentucky, Tennessee.

A sad bride makes a glad wife. **[31]**
  Kin, p. 34.
  Mieder, Dic., p. 70, #2, Illinois.
Saith Solomon the wise, "A good wife is a good prize." **[28]**
  Loomis, GE, p. 196, #1. (1866)
The same flowers that adorn a bride are placed on a corpse. **[31]**
  Kin, p. 97.
The second wife always sits on the right knee. **[28]**
  Thompson, p. 484, New York.
  Mieder, Dic., p. 654, #38, New York. (1940)
See how the boy is with his sister and you can know how the man will
be with your daughter. **[58]**
  Zona, p. 58, Plains Sioux.
See your sons and daughter: they are your future. **[58]**
  Zona, p. 58, Oneida.
A sensible wife looks for her enjoyment at "home"—a silly one,
"abroad." **[28]**
  Hines, p. 286, Pacific Northwest.
Shame in a woman is known by her dress. **[49]**
  West, p. 42, Mexican-American. (1963)
She drove her ducks to a poor market. [She made a bad marriage.]
  Brewster, FSI, p. 263, Indiana. (1939)
She has on a brand splinterfire new dress. **[49]**
  Atkinson, p. 83, Texas.
  Boatwright, p. 216, Texas.
She likes anything that wears pants. **[65]**
  Person, p. 180, #151, Washington.
She's flirting like a Spanish filly. **[65]**
  Atkinson, p. 83, Texas.
  Boatwright, p. 216, Texas.
She's got her cap set for him. **[65]**
  Brewster, FSI, p. 263, Indiana. (1939)
She's one of the old blue hen's chickens. [a hellcat, a termagant] **[39]**
  Atkinson, p. 83, Texas.
She's painted up like a wild Indian. **[49]**
  Atkinson, p. 83, Texas.
She that hath a bad husband hath a hell within her own house. **[28]**
  Loomis, GE, p. 198, #54. (1866)
She that hath an ill husband shows it in her dress. **[28]**
  Brown, p. 109.
  Loomis, GE, p. 198, #55. (1866)
She tried it on at first, saying your presence, sir, by going to bed missus
and getting up master. **[28]**

Taylor and Whiting, p. 247, #2.

She wants to be the bride at every wedding and the corpse at every funeral. **[39]**

Person, p. 180, #126, Washington.

She was melted and poured into her dress. **[49]**

Clark, p. 162, #421, North Carolina.

She was pure as the snow, but she drifted. **[102]**

Thompson, p. 493, New York.

She wears the trousers. **[85]**

Yoffie, p. 149, #205. (Yiddish)

She who dresses in black must rely on her beauty. **[49]**

Mieder, AP, p. 63. (Mexican-American)

She who is born beautiful is born married. **[49]**

(*Variation 1*: She that is born a beauty, is born half-married.)

(*Variation 2*: She who is a beauty is half married; She who is born beautiful is half married.)

Kin, p. 22.

Loomis, GE, p. 197, #19. ("handsome" for "beautiful") (1866)

(1. Kin, p. 282.)

(1. Loomis, FA, p. 174.) (1798)

(1. Loomis, GE, p. 197, #18.) (1866)

(2. Mieder, Dic., p. 41, #38, Illinois, New York, Vermont) (1732) (English)

She who marries a man for his money, will have the man but not the money. **[28]**

Person, p. 178, #67, Washington.

She won't do it with anybody but a friend—and she ain't got an enemy in the world. [said of a girl with loose morals] **[102]**

Brewster, SAB, p. 156, Indiana. (1944)

Shinin' like a gal's face when she's a fixin' to be married. **[31]**

Taylor and Whiting, p. 126, #11.

A ship and a woman are ever repairing. **[70]**

(*Variation 1*: A ship and a woman always want trimming.)

(*Variation 2*: A ship, a mill and a woman are always repairing.)

[*See also*: Old houses and old ladies always need repairing.]

Kin, p. 282.

Brown, p. 98. (Scottish)

(1. Brown, p. 48.)

(2. Loomis, FA, p. 173.) (1795) (English, 1670)

A ship under sail and a big-bellied woman are the handsomest two things that can be seen (common). **[71]**

Franklin, 1735.

Kin, p. 198. (common) [under pregnancy]

Mieder, Dic., 535, #3, New York, South Carolina. (1609) (English)

The Shoemaker's wife goes barefoot. **[28]**
   (*Variation 1*: Shoemakers' wives are the worst shod.)
   (*Variation 2*: The smith's mare and the cobbler's wife are always the worst shod.)
   Hardie, p. 464, #135.
   (1. Brown, p. 131.)
   (2. Kin, p. 173.)
Silence is a fine jewel for a woman, but it is little worn. **[89]**
   (*Variation*: "veil" for "jewel"
   Kin, p. 234.
   Mieder, Dic., p. 540, #5, Illinois. (1539)
   (Loomis, FA, p. 173.) (1795) (Irish)
A simple maiden in her flower is worth a hundred coats-of-arms. **[39]**
   Kin, p. 271. [under virginity]
A skinny woman's like a racehorse: fast and fun, but no good for work. **[71]**
   Mieder, Dic., p. 665, #2, New Mexico.
Slander expires at a good woman's door. **[79]**
   Kin, p. 237.
   Mieder, Dic., p. 545, #1, Illinois.
A small sprinkling of the feminine gender, just enough to take the cuss off, and no more. **[39]**
   Taylor and Whiting, p. 88, #5.
Smelt as sweet as a gal's breath. **[39]**
   Taylor and Whiting, p. 42, breath.
The smiles of a pretty woman are the tears of the purse. **[49]**
   (*Variation*: When a handsome woman laughs you may be sure her purse weeps.)
   Kin, p. 252.
   (Thiselton-Dyer, p. 230.) (Italian)
A smoky chimney and a scolding wife are two bad companions. **[71]**
   Kin, p. 46.
   Mieder, Dic., p. 98, #1, Illinois.
The society of ladies is a school of politeness. **[112]**
   Loomis, GE, p. 197, #36. (1866)
So dishonest he'd steal his grandmother's false teeth. **[109]**
   Person, p. 183, #261, Washington.
So long as woman is on friendly terms with modesty just so long is woman vindicated and no longer. **[79]**
   Hines, p. 292, Pacific Northwest.
Some say she do, and some say she don't. **[102]**
   Kin, p. 67. [under doubt]
Spit in a whore's face and she'll say it's raining. **[93]**
   Kin, p. 279.

Mieder, Dic., p. 652, #2, Illinois.

Spring is the time when a young man's fancy turns to what a young woman has been thinking all winter. [65]

Thompson, p. 493, New York.

Mieder, Dic., p. 559, #3b. ["the whole year" for "all winter"] (1842)

A squaw's tongue runs faster than the wind's legs. [89]

Kin, p. 282.

"Indian Proverbs," p. 173.

Mieder, AP, p. 106, Oklahoma.

Mieder, PNA, p. 258.

Step on a crack, break your mother's back. [56]

Titelman, p. 307. [bad luck]

Strong men of arms become like putty in the arms of women. [65]

Kin, p. 14.

Stupidity in a woman is unfeminine. [39]

Kin, p. 265.

Swine, women and bees cannot be turned. [71]

(*Variation*: Swine, women and bees, none o' these can ye turn.)

Loomis, FA, p. 173. (1796)

(Brown, p. 72, Connecticut.)

Take a friend for what he does, a wife for what she has, and goods for what they are worth. [28]

Mieder, Dic., p. 238, #151, Illinois, Ohio.

Talking women sound like chickens eating scratch feed on a tin roof. [89]

Clark, p. 172, #701, North Carolina.

A taught horse, a woman to teach, and teachers practicing what they preach. [71]

Franklin, 1733.

Tell a woman and you tell the world. [89]

Mieder, Dic., p. 667, #57. (1700)

Tell a woman she's a beauty and the devil will tell her it ten times. [49]

(*Variation*: Once tell a woman she's a beauty and the devil will tell her so ten times.)

Kin, p. 282.

Mieder, Dic., p. 667, #58, Illinois. (1732)

(Brown, p. 111.) (Spanish, Italian)

Ten measures of talk were sent down from heaven, and women took nine. [89]

Mieder, Dic., p. 581, #12.

That's the reason deacons' sons seldom turn out well, and preachers' daughters are married through a window. [eloped] [58]

Taylor and Whiting, p. 94, #3.

That woman is young that does not look a day older than she says she is. **[49]**

  [*See also*: A woman is as old as she admits.]

  [*See also*: A woman is as old as she looks.]

  Mieder, Dic., p. 667, #59, Mississippi.

There are as many good step-mothers as white ravens. **[56]**

  Kin, p. 243.

  Mieder, Dic., p. 563, Illinois. (1640)

There are men who go to a gymnasium for exercise while their wives are sawing the wood. **[28]**

  Hines, p. 211, Pacific Northwest.

There are three classes of people one must not provoke: officials, customers and widows. **[105]**

  Kin, p. 179.

There are three faithful friends—an old wife, an old dog, and ready money. **[71]**

  Franklin, 1738.

  Kin, p. 101.

  Mieder, Dic., p. 239, #166, Illinois, Indiana, Wisconsin.

There are three things it takes a strong man to hold—a young warrior, a wild horse, and a handsome squaw. **[71]**

  "Indian Proverbs," p. 173.

  Mieder, AP, p. 106, Oklahoma.

There are two kinds of women: those who take what you are and those who take what you have. **[39]**

  Mieder, Dic., p. 668, #71, New Jersey, North Carolina.

There is little peace in that house where the hen crows and the cock is mute. **[112]**

  Kin, p. 233.

There is many a good wife that can't sing and dance well. **[28]**

  Brown, p. 110. [who cannot]

  Loomis, GE, p. 196, #4. (1866)

There is no mischief but a woman is at the heart of it. **[39]**

  (*Variation*: There is no mischief in the world done, but a woman is always one.)

  Kin, p. 281.

  (Loomis, GE, p. 197, #25.) (1866)

There is no such thing as a bad mother. **[56]**

  Coffin and Cohen, p. 145. (Yiddish)

  Yoffie, p. 147, #183. (Yiddish)

There is nothing better than a good woman and nothing worse than a bad one. **[79]**

  Mieder, Dic., p. 668, #72, New York. (1948)

There is one good wife in the country, and every man thinks he hath her. **[29]**

> Loomis, GE, p. 197, #46. (1866)

There is only one good mother-in-law, and she is dead. **[56]**

> Brown, p. 115. ("but" for "and")
> Kin, p. 169.

There is somethin' wus than galls in the bushes. **[122]**

> Taylor and Whiting, p. 152, #10.

There never was a mirror (looking glass) that told a woman she was ugly. **[50]**

> (*Variation*: Never a looking glass told a woman she was ugly.)
> Kin, p. 263. (French)
> (Hines, p. 194, Pacific Northwest.)

There's hardly a strife in which a woman has not been a prime mover. **[112]**

> Kin, p. 282.
> Mieder, Dic., p. 668, #74, Illinois, Oregon. (1658)

There's no accounting for the actions of women. **[97]**

> Kin, p. 282.

There's not a pretty girl without fault, nor an ugly one without charm. **[50]**

> West, p. 43, Mexican-American. (1963)

There was never a conflict without a woman. **[112]**

> Mieder, Dic., p. 668, #73, Wisconsin. (1639)

They all know what to do with a bad wife but he who's got one. **[29]**

> Mieder, Dic., p. 654, #40, Utah. (1621)

Thorns and thistles sting very sure, but old maids' tongues sting more. **[94]**

> Kin, p. 244.

Thou lovest thine own will; but as for that matter show me the woman that does not. **[39]**

> Hines, p. 287, Pacific Northwest.

Three kinds of men can't understand women: young men, old men, and middle-aged men. **[122]**

> Kin, p. 264.

The three merriest things under the sun: A cat's kitten, A goat's kid, And a young widow. **[105]**

> Whiting, PPNC, p. 345, North Carolina. (Irish)

Three things are as rare as gold: a good melon, a good friend, and a good wife. **[71]**

> Kin, p. 109.

Three things are men most likely to be cheated in: a horse, a wig and a wife. **[71]**

> Franklin, 1736.

Three without rule—A mule, A pig, A woman. (Irish) **[71]**

(Variation 1: Three things that will have their way—a lass, a pig, and an ass.)

(Variation 2: The three most difficult to teach—a woman, a pig, and a mule.) (English)

Whiting, PPNC, p. 345, North Carolina. (original and variations)
Three women and a goose make a market. **[89]**

(Variation: Three men and one hog make a market.)

Loomis, GE, p. 198, #57. (1866)

(Loomis, GE, p. 198, #58.) (1866)
Thrift is to a man what chastity is to a woman. **[39]**

Mieder, Dic., p. 594, #3, New York, South Carolina. (1937)
To go through [something] like a dose of salts through a woman. **[122]**

(Variations for "a woman": hired girl; tall Swede.)

Barbour, p. 296, #26, Illinois.
To hunt out a wife as one goes to Smithfield for a horse. **[71]**

Whiting, EA, p. 482, W154. (1775)
Too much whiskey will kill; too many women will chill. **[40]**

Kin, p. 170.
To smell like a whorehouse on Saturday night. **[93]**

Taylor, PCSC, p. 88.
To win the lady, first bribe her maid. **[65]**

Kin, p. 34.
The treasure of a woman is her virtue. **[79]**

West, p. 42, Mexican-American. (1962)
True man does not know woman, but neither does woman. **[97]**

Brown, p. 114.
A true wife is her husband's better half. **[29]**

(Variation 1: A true wife is her husband's flower of beauty.)

(Variation 2: A true wife is her husband's heart's treasure.)

Mieder, Dic., p. 653, #10 Mississippi.

(1. Mieder, Dic., p. 653, #11, Mississippi.)

(2. Mieder, Dic., p. 653, #12, Mississippi.)
A true wife is proud of her husband; he, the calves of his legs. **[29]**

Hines, p. 286, Pacific Northwest.
Trust your dog to the end, and a woman to the first opportunity. **[97]**

Kin, p. 282.
A truth-telling woman finds few friends. **[122]**

Hines, p. 292, Pacific Northwest. (Danish)
Twice is a woman dear; when she comes to the house and when she leaves it. **[122]**

Hines, p. 292, Pacific Northwest.
A two-faced woman and a jealous man is the cause of trouble since the world began. **[65]**

Mieder, Dic., p. 665, #3, Wisconsin.

Two good days for a man in his life: when he weds, and when he buries his wife. [29]
    Kin, p. 35.
Two things govern the world—women and gold. [112]
    Mieder, Dic., p. 668, #75, Oregon.
Two women in the same house can never agree. [117]
    (*Variation*: Two women in one house, two cats and one mouse, two dogs and one bone, will never accord.)
    [*See also*: No house is big enough for two women.]
    Mieder, Dic., p. 668, #76. (1417)
    (Brown, p. 111.)
The ugliest girl makes the best housewife. [50]
    Kin, p. 123.
The ugliest woman can look in the mirror and think she is beautiful. [50]
    Mieder, Dic., p. 668, #66, North Carolina. (1948)
Ugliness is the guardian of women. [50]
    Kin, p. 263.
    Mieder, Dic., p. 623, Illinois. (Hebrew)
An ugly baby makes a pretty girl. [50]
    Mieder, AP, p. 90, North Carolina.
An ugly man never gets a pretty wife. [50]
    Mieder, Dic., p. 623, #2, North Carolina.
An ugly woman dreads the mirror. [50]
    Kin, p. 263.
    Mieder, Dic., p. 623, #3, Illinois. (Japanese)
The unchaste woman can never become chaste again. [78]
    Kin, p. 264.
    Mieder, Dic., p. 623, #1, Illinois.
The unchaste woman will hesitate at no wickedness. [78]
    Kin, p. 264.
    Mieder, Dic., p. 623, #2, Illinois.
An undutiful daughter will prove an unmanageable wife. [58]
    Franklin, 1752.
    Mieder, Dic., p. 135, #2, New Jersey. (1862) (Scottish)
Vanity acts like a woman—they both think they lose something when love or praise is accorded to another. [50]
    Hines, p. 278, Pacific Northwest.
    [*See also*: Frailty, your name is woman.]
    [*See also*: Woman, thy name is curiosity.]
Vanity, thy name is woman. [50]
    Hines, p. 278, Pacific Northwest.
Virgins uv forty-five . . . tough ez wire. [102]
    Taylor and Whiting, p. 407, #1.
A virtuous woman is a source of honor to her husband; a vicious one causes him disgrace. [79]

(*Variation*: A virtuous woman is a crown to her husband.) [from Proverbs xii.4 . . . but she that maketh ashamed is as rottenness to his house.]
Mieder, Dic., p. 665, #4, Illinois.
(Brown, p. 109.)
A virtuous woman is rarer than a precious jewel. [80]
Mieder, Dic., p. 634, #2, North Carolina.
A virtuous woman, though ugly, is the ornament of the house. [80]
Loomis, GE, p. 196, #2. (1866)
Vivacity is the gift of woman. [40]
Kin, p. 272.
Mieder, Dic., p. 635, #3, Illinois.
Want makes strife between man and wife. [29]
Kin, p. 274.
Mieder, Dic., p. 638, #6, Illinois. (1732)
A warm-back husband and a cold-foot wife should easily lead a compatible life. [29]
Mieder, TLSM, p. 55, Vermont.
Weeping like a girl. [40]
Brunvand, Dic., p. 58.
What a woman does not know she imagines. [97]
[*See also*: An old maid doesn't know anything but what she imagines.]
Brown, p. 113.
What a woman has to say above a whisper isn't worth listening to. [85]
Mieder, Dic., p. 668, #77, New Jersey.
What ever women do they must do twice as well as men to be thought half as good. Luckily, this is not difficult. [Charlotte Whitton] [40]
Adams, A., p. 160.
What woman wills God wills. [112]
Hines, p. 292, Pacific Northwest. (French)
When a girl whistles, the angels cry. [85]
Mieder, Dic., p. 251, #20, New York.
When a man's a fool, his wife will rule. [29]
Mieder, Dic., p. 225, #170.
When a man takes a wife, he ceases to dread hell. [29]
Mieder, Dic., p. 404, #235, California.
When a woman is speaking, listen to what she says with her eyes. [89]
Mieder, Dic., p. 668, #78, New York.
When a woman reigns, the devil governs. [112]
Hines, p. 292, Pacific Northwest. (Italian)
Kin, p. 297.
When a woman throws a man over, he usually lands on his knees to another woman. [65]
Mieder, Dic., p. 668, #79, Mississippi.
When ladies wear the breeches, their petticoats ought to be long enough to hide 'em. [85]

Mieder, Dic., p. 359, #12, New York, South Carolina.

Taylor and Whiting, p. 42, Breeches.

When mothers-in-law fall out, then we get at the family facts. [57]

Hines, p. 216, Pacific Northwest. (Spanish)

When the cask is full the mother-in-law gets drunk. [57]

Kin, p. 41.

When the good man is from home, the good wife's table is soon spread.
[29]

Loomis, GE, p. 197, #28. (1866)

When the housewife is a slattern, the cat is a glutton. [117]

Yoffie, p. 141, #87. (Yiddish)

When the husband earns well, the wife spends well. [29]

Mieder, Dic., p. 320, #19, Wisconsin.

When the husband's away, the wife will play. [29]

Mieder, AP, p. 93, Tennessee.

When the stars fall agin maybe the women will be harmonized. [therefore
never] [97]

Taylor and Whiting, p. 350, #8.

When the wife dies and the mare foals, prosperity begins. [71]

Kin, p. 156.

When the wife rules the house, the devil is man-servant. [113]

Kin, p. 156.

When women are on board there is no want of wind. [89]

Mieder, AP, p. 45. (American)

Mieder, Enc., p. 543, #17998.

Whiting, EA, p. 493, W275. (1789)

When you choose a wife, shut your eyes and commend your soul to God.
[29]

Hines, p. 286, Pacific Northwest. (Spanish)

When you get one girl you better try two, cause there ain't no telling
what one'll do. [65]

Mieder, Dic., p. 251, #21, Alabama, Georgia.

Wherever there is a woman, there is gossip. [89]

Mieder, Dic., p. 668, #80, West Virginia.

Where the cobwebs grow; The beaux don't go. [Girls who aren't good
housekeepers won't attract husbands.] [117]

Mieder, TLSM, p. 53, Vermont.

Person, p. 179, #84, Washington. [no "the's"]

Smith and Eddins, p. 240, Texas.

Thompson, p. 483, New York.

Where there is no wife there is no home. [29]

Mieder, Dic., p. 654, #41.

Where there's a woman, there's trouble. [from the French "cherchez la
femme" or "look for the woman"] [40]

Whiting, MPPS, p. 693.
Where there's a world it's woman that will govern it. **[115]**
(*Variation*: While there's a world, it's a woman that will govern it.)
Kin, p. 281.
(Mieder, Dic., p. 668, #81, Illinois.)
Where women and geese are there is no lack of noise. **[89]**
Hines, p. 294, Pacific Northwest. (English)
While the tall maid is stooping, the little one has swept the house. **[117]**
Loomis, GE, p. 197, #34. (1866)
The whisper of a pretty girl can be heard further than the roar of a lion.
[65]
Mieder, Dic., p. 251, #19, Wisconsin.
A whistling girl and a crowing hen; Always come to some bad end. **[85]**
(*Variation 1*: A whistling woman and a crowing hen are two of the
unluckiest things on earth.)
(*Variation 2*: A whistling woman and a crowing hen; Are neither fit for
God or men.)
(*Variation 3*: A whistling girl and a cackling hen come to no good end.)
(*Variation 4*: Girls who (that) whistle and hens that crow, Should have
their necks twisted betimes.)
(*Variation 5*: The girl that whistles or a hen that crows always catch
the nicest beaux.)
(*Variation 6*: A whistling girl and a crowing hen; Are sure to come to
some bad end.)
Adams, MCP, p. 140, #74, California.
Mieder, AP, p. 86, Louisiana.
Mieder, Dic., p. 651, #1. [There are 13 variations.] (1721) (English,
Scottish)
Whiting, PPNC, p. 345, North Carolina. [There are 12 variations.]
(1. Brown, p. 37.)
(2. Whiting, PPNC, pp. 345–46.) (English)
(3. Pearce, New Mexico.)
(4. Hoffman, p. 198, #12, Pennsylvania German.)
(5. Welsch, p. 270, Nebraska.)
(6. Smith and Eddins, p. 239, Texas.)
A whistling girl and an old black sheep; Are the only things a farmer can
keep. **[71]**
(*Variation 1*: A whistling girl and a bleating sheep; Are the best stock
a farmer can keep.)
(*Variation 2*: Whistling girls and jumping sheep; Are the poorest property a man can keep.)
(*Variation 3*. Whistling girls and jumping sheep always come to the
top of the heap.)
[Six more variations on the same theme using a flock of sheep, a good

fat sheep, and an old black sheep can be found in Mieder, Dic., p. 651, #2.]

Whiting, PPNC, p. 346, North Carolina.

(1. Whiting, PPNC, p. 346.) (English)

(2. Person, p. 179, #97, Washington.)

(3. Mieder, TLSM, p. 51, Vermont.)

Who finds a wife finds a good thing. [29]

Mieder, Dic., p. 654, #42, New York. (1948)

Who has a bad wife, has purgatory for a neighbor. [29]

Loomis, GE, p. 198, #53. (1866)

Who is the wife of one cannot eat the rice of two. [29]

Mieder, Dic., p. 654, #43, Indiana.

Whores' curses are blessings. [93]

Kin, p. 279.

Mieder, Dic., p. 652, #3, Illinois. (1855) (English)

The widow gave orders to her cat and the cat gave them to its tail. [105]

Kin, p. 222. [under runaround]

A widow is a boat without a rudder. [105]

Kin, p. 29. (Chinese)

A widow is known by her weeds, a man for his deeds. [105]

Kin, p. 66.

Widows who cry easily are the first to marry again. There is nothing like wet weather for transplanting. [106]

Hendricks, p. 92, Texas. [attributed to Oliver Wendell Holmes] [106]

Widows will be widows.

Mieder, AP, p. 44. (American)

Mieder, Enc., p. 525, #17335.

A wife can make or break her husband. [financially] [30]

Yoffie, p. 149, #203. (Yiddish)

Wife, from thy spouse each blemish hide, more than from all the world beside. [30]

Kin, p. 279.

A wife is a young man's slave and an old man's darling. [30]

(Variation 1: Better be an old man's darling than a young man's slave [warling].)

(Variation 2: It is better to be an old man's darling, than a poor man's slave.)

Mieder, Dic., p. 653, #13, Illinois. (1546) (English)

(1. Kin, p. 55.)

(1. Mieder, TLSM, p. 50, Vermont.)

(2. Welsch, p. 266, Nebraska.)

A wife is not to be chosen by the eye only. [65]

[See also: Choose a wife rather by your ear than your eye.]

Loomis, FA, p. 174. (1797)

A wife is seen with the greatest pleasure by her husband in two circumstances only, at the wedding and in the winding sheet. [30]
  Whiting, EA, p. 482, W155. (Greek) (1786)
The wife is the keeper of her husband's conscience as well as his soul. [30]
  Kin, p. 157.
Wife, make thine own candle, Spare penny to handle. [thrifty] [30]
  Thompson, p. 487, New York.
  Mieder, Dic., p. 654, #44, New York. (1940)
The wife who loves the looking-glass hates the saucepan. [30]
  [See also: The more women look in their glass the less they look in their house.]
  Kin, p. 151.
Wine and women don't mix. [72]
  Mieder, Dic., p. 658, #14, Alabama, Georgia.
Wine, women and song will get a man wrong. [72]
  Mieder, Dic., p. 658, #22, North Carolina. (1580) (English)
Winter weather and women's thoughts change often. [98]
  Brown, p. 92. [often change]
  Kin, p. 280.
  Mieder, Dic., p. 659, #9, Illinois. (1450)
A wise woman is twice a fool. [85]
  Kin, p. 280.
A wise woman never outsmarts her husband. [85]
  Mieder, AP, p. 85, Kansas.
  Mieder, Dic., p. 661, #20, New York.
A wolf is handsome in the eyes of a lovesick girl. [65]
  Kin, p. 115.
A woman, a cat, and a chimney should never leave the house. [72]
  Mieder, Dic., p. 665, #5, Texas.
  Smith and Eddins, p. 240, Texas.
A woman, a dog and a walnut tree: the more you beat them, the better they be. [72]
  (Variation 1: A wife and a walnut tree, the more you beat them, the better they be.)
  (Variation 2: A spaniel, a woman, and a walnut tree, The more they be beaten, the better they be.)
  (Variation 3: A woman, a dog, and a hickory tree: the more you beat them, the more they beg.)
  (Variation 4: A woman, a dog, and a walnut tree: the harder you beat 'em, the better they be.)
  (Variation 5: A woman, a dog, and a walnut tree: the worse you treat them, the better they will be.)
  (Variation 6: "spaniel" for "dog")

Brown, p. 110. [the more they're beaten, the better they'll be.]
Mieder, Dic., p. 665, #6. (1581)
Taylor and Whiting, p. 408, #1. ["lick 'em" for "beat them"]
(1. Brown, p. 67)
(2. Kin, p. 22)
(3. Mieder, Dic., p. 665, #6a.)
(4. Mieder, Dic., p. 665, #6b.)
(4. Smith and Eddins, p. 240, Texas.)
(5. Mieder, Dic., p. 665, #6c.)
(6. Whiting, MPPS, p. 694.)

The woman always pays. [122]
Whiting, MPPS, pp. 694–95.

A woman always thinks it takes two to keep a secret. [89]
Kin, p. 227.

A woman and a cherry are painted for their own harm. [50]
Mieder, Dic., p. 665, #7, Michigan. (1659) (Spanish)

A woman and a greyhound must be small in the waist. [72]
Loomis, GE, p. 197, #11. (1866) (Spanish)

Woman at her housework that's what women are for. [85]
West, p. 42, Mexican-American.

Woman brings to man the greatest blessing and the greatest plague. [40]
Kin, p. 282.
Mieder, Dic., p. 668, #82, Illinois. (1948)

A woman can never keep a secret. [89]
Taylor and Whiting, p. 409, #5.
Whiting, MPPS, p. 694. ["cannot" for "can never"]

A woman can play the deuce [devil] with a fellow. [40]
Brunvand, Dic., p. 35.

A woman can't drive her husband, but she can lead him. [85]
Mieder, Dic., p. 666, #9, New York.

A woman conceals what she knows not. [40]
Brown, p. 111.
Hines, p. 289, Pacific Northwest. (does not know) (French)
Loomis, GE, p. 197, #31. (1866) (that)
Mieder, Dic., p. 666, #10, Oklahoma, Texas. (1386, Chaucer)

A woman convinced against her will; Is of the same opinion still. [40]
Mieder, Dic., p. 358, #3, Kansas, Ohio. [Also: A lady persuaded . . .]
Whiting, PPNC, p. 345, North Carolina.

A woman could throw out with a spoon faster than a man could throw in with a shovel. [98]

(*Variation 1*: A wasteful woman throws out with a spoon faster than her husband can fetch in with a shovel.)

(*Variation 2*: A wasteful wife throws out in the dishwater more'n her husband can tote in.)

(*Variation 3*: She throwed more out the backdoor than her old man could tote in the front.)

(*Variation 4*: A woman can throw away more [food] with a spoon than a man can bring in with a shovel.)

(*Variation 5*: A woman can throw out more with a spoon than a man can bring home with a shovel.)

Taylor and Whiting, p. 409, #7.

Thompson, p. 487, New York.

(1, 2, and 3. Whiting, PPNC, p. 345, North Carolina.)

(4. Brewster, FSI, p. 265, Indiana.)

(5. Mieder, TLSM, p. 50, Vermont.)

A woman doesn't worry as much over how she is to gain a crown of glory as she does how she is to gain a new bonnet. [50]

Hines, p. 289, Pacific Northwest.

A woman don't know her own mind half an hour together. [98]

Whiting, EA, p. 494, W286. (1771)

A woman fights with her tongue. [90]

Mieder, Dic., p. 666, #11.

Woman: God bless her by that name, for it is a far nobler name than lady. [122]

Mieder, Dic., p. 668, #83, New York. (1931)

A woman has never spoiled anything through silence. [90]

Kin, p. 234. (German)

A woman is a dish for the gods. [72]

Mieder, Dic., p. 666, #12, New Jersey.

A woman is always grateful to you—for having thrown you overboard. [65]

Hines, p. 290, Pacific Northwest.

Woman is a mystery to men but women are wise to each other. [122]

Kin, p. 282.

Mieder, Dic., p. 668, #84, Illinois.

A woman is as old as she admits. [50]

(Variation: A man is as old as he feels, a woman as old as she feels like admitting.)

[*See also*: That woman is young that does not look a day older than she says she is.]

[*See also*: A woman is as old as she looks.]

Kin, p. 8.

(Titelman, p. 227.) (1871) (American, 1926).

A woman is as old as she looks. (A man is old when he quits looking.) [50]

(*Variation 1*: A woman is no older than she looks.)

(*Variation 2*: A woman is no older than she looks, and a man than he feels.)

(*Variation 3*: A man is as old as he feels, and a woman as old as she looks.)

[*See also*: That woman is young that does not look a day older than she says she is.]

[*See also*: A woman is as old as she admits.]

Bradley, p. 98, South Carolina.

(1 and 2. Mieder, Dic., p. 666, #15, Alabama, Georgia, Texas.)

(3. Adams, TPSFC, p. 62, #72, California.)

(3. Mieder, AP, p. 80, California.)

(3. Mieder, TLSM p. 54, Vermont.)

Woman is as variable as a feather in the wind. [98]

Kin, p. 268.

A woman is at the bottom of every lawsuit. [40]

(*Variation*: There is scarcely a lawsuit unless a woman is the cause of it.) [from Juvenal]

Kin, p. 145.

Woman is a weathercock (turning vane). [unsteadfast] [98]

Whiting, MPPS, p. 695. (English)

A woman is known by her walking and drinking. [40]

Kin, p. 274.

Mieder, Dic., p. 666, #14, New York. (Spanish)

A woman is like your shadow; follow her she flies; fly from her, she follows. [65]

(*Variation*: Flee, and she follows; follow, and she'll flee.)

Hines, p. 290, Pacific Northwest.

(Kin, p. 282.)

A woman is only a woman. (A good cigar is a smoke) [72]

Mieder, Dic., p. 666, #16, California, Michigan, Oregon.

A woman is seldom tenderer to a man than immediately after she has deceived him. [78]

Hines, p. 290, Pacific Northwest.

A woman is the greatest contradiction of all. [40]

(*Variation*: Woman at best is a contradiction still.) [from Alexander Pope's "Moral Essays"]

Mieder, Dic., p. 666, #17, Illinois.

(Hines, p. 289, Pacific Northwest.)

Woman is the key to life's mystery. [40]

Kin, p. 139.

Woman is woe to man. [40]

Whiting, EA, p. 493, W279. (1700)

A woman knows a bit more than Satan. [40]

Mieder, Dic., p. 666, #18, Illinois. (1559)

Woman learns how to hate when she has lost the ability to charm. [40]

Brown, p. 114.

A woman listens to a play with her mind and judges it with her senses.
[41]
  Hines, p. 290, Pacific Northwest.
A woman must be wooed and won. [65]
  Bradley, p. 98, South Carolina.
Woman must have her way. [41]
  (*Variation 1*: A woman will always have her way.)
  (*Variation 2*: Woman will have both her word and her way.)
  (*Variation 3*: Man has his will, but woman has her way.)
  (*Variation 4*: A woman has her way.)
  (*Variation 5*: Women will have their way.)
  Kin, p. 282.
  Mieder, Dic., p. 668, #85, Illinois, New York.
  (1. Taylor and Whiting, p. 409, #2.)
  (2 and 3. Mieder, Dic., p. 668, #85, Illinois, New York.)
  (4. Whiting, MPPS, p. 694.)
  (5. Whiting, EA, p. 495, W292.) (1774)
A woman need not always recall her age, but she should never forget it.
[51]
  Hines, p. 290, Pacific Northwest.
A woman never forgets her sex. She would rather talk with a man than
an angel any day. [102]
  Mieder, Dic., p. 666, #20, Wisconsin. (1872)
A woman never holds her tongue: but when she's contriving mischief.
[90]
  Whiting, EA, p. 494, W280. (1720)
A woman over thirty who will tell her exact age will tell anything. [51]
  Mieder, Dic., p. 666, #21, New York.
A woman remembers a kiss long after a man has forgotten. [65]
  Mieder, Dic., p. 666, #22, New York.
Woman rules man, but de debil rules her. [113]
  Brunvand, Dic., p. 154.
  Mieder, AP, p. 84, Indiana. (the devil)
A woman's bonnet must be orthodox before her prayer-book is. [51]
  Hines, p. 290, Pacific Northwest.
A woman's excuses are like her apron, easily lifted. [98]
  Whiting, PPNC, p. 345, North Carolina. (English)
A woman's fame is the tomb of her happiness. [85]
  Hines, p. 290, Pacific Northwest.
A woman's friendship is, as a rule, the legacy of love or the alms of
indifference. [41]
  Hines, p. 291, Pacific Northwest.
A woman's hair is her crowning glory. [51]
  Mieder, Dic., p. 666, #25, New York. (1948)

A woman's hair is long; her tongue is longer. [90]
Mieder, Dic., p. 666, #26, Oregon.
Woman—she shares our griefs, doubles our joys, and trebles our expenses. [41]
Hines, p. 289, Pacific Northwest.
A woman should hang on to her youth, but not while he's driving. [122]
Mieder, Dic., p. 666, #23, North Dakota.
A woman's in pain, a woman's in woe; a woman is ill when she likes to be so. [98]
Kin, p. 156. [under malingerer]
Mieder, Dic., p. 666, #27, North Dakota. (Italian)
A woman spins even while she talks. [41]
Kin, p. 233. [under shrewdness]
A woman's place is in the home. [85]
(Variation 1: "hay" for "home"
(Variation 2: Woman's sphere is in the home.)
Mieder, Dic., p. 666, #28. (1844) (original and both variations.)
Taylor and Whiting, p. 409, #9.
Whiting, MPPS, p. 695. ["the" for "her"]
A woman's strength is in her tongue. [90]
Mieder, Dic., p. 666, #29, Ohio. (1659) (English)
A woman's strongest weapons are her tears. [41]
Hines, p. 291, Pacific Northwest.
A woman's tears are a fountain of craft. [41]
Hines, p. 290, Pacific Northwest. (English)
A woman's tongue is only three inches long, but it can kill a man six feet high. [90]
Kin, p. 257. (Japanese)
A woman's tongue is sharper than a double-edged sword. [90]
Mieder, TLSM, p. 51, Vermont.
A woman's tongue wags like a lamb's tail. [90]
Kin, p. 143.
A woman's vengeance knows no bounds. [41]
Kin, p. 268. (German)
A woman's whole life is a history of the affections. [41]
Mieder, Dic., p. 666, #30, New York.
A woman's wit is a help. [122]
Whiting, MPPS, p. 695.
The woman that deliberates is lost. [85]
Kin, p. 253.
Mieder, Dic., p. 668, #67, New Jersey. (1713)
Taylor and Whiting, p. 409, #6. ("calc'lates" for "deliberates")
A woman that loves to be at the windows is like a bunch of grapes in the highway. [41]

Loomis, FA, p. 176. (1804)
Woman thy name is curiosity. [41]
　　[See also: Frailty, your name is woman.]
　　[See also: Vanity, thy name is woman.]
　　Whiting, EA, p. 494, W282. (1775)
The woman to whom you give what she asks for, is the woman who will
give you what you ask for. [122]
　　West, pp. 42–43, Mexican-American. (1962)
Woman was placed on earth to show men both paradise and purgatory.
[86]
　　Brown, p. 113.
The woman who confides to one man her partiality for another seeks
advice less than avowal. [66]
　　Hines, p. 290, Pacific Northwest.
The woman who dresses in silk stays at home. [51]
　　West, p. 42, Mexican-American. (1963)
The woman who dresses in yellow trusts her beauty. [51]
　　West, p. 42, Mexican-American. (1963)
The woman who likes washing can always find water. [41]
　　Kin, p. 275.
The woman who'll kiss and tell is small as the little end of nothing. [66]
　　Mieder, Dic., p. 668, #68, New York.
A woman who looks much in the glass spins but little. [51]
　　Mieder, Dic., p. 666, #24, Wisconsin. (1623)
A woman will refuse and then accept. [98]
　　[See also: Between a woman's yes and a woman's no; there's not
enough room for a pin to go.]
　　[See also: Girls say no when they mean yes.]
　　Whiting, EA, p. 494, W281. (1733)
A woman without a man is like a handle without a pan. [41]
　　Loomis, GE, p. 196, #8. (1867)
A woman without religion is a flower without perfume. A man without
religion is a horse without a bridle. [41]
　　Kin, p. 213.
Woman would be more charming if one could fall into her arms without
falling into her hands. [66]
　　Brown, p. 114.
　　Mieder, Dic., p. 669, #105, Wisconsin. [plural] (1929)
A woman would sooner rule a heart than fill it; not so a man. [66]
　　Hines, p. 290, Pacific Northwest.
The woman you keep keeps you. [122]
　　Kin, p. 282.
　　Mieder, Dic., p. 668, #69, Illinois.
Women and dogs cause too much strife. [72]

Mieder, Dic., p. 668, #86, Mississippi, New York. (1541)

Women and dogs set men together by the ears. [41]
  Kin, p. 281.
  Mieder, Dic., p. 668, #87, Illinois, New York. (1639)

Women and elephants never forget. [41]
  Kin, p. 281.
  Mieder, Dic., p. 668, #88, Illinois. (1910)

Women and glass are always in danger. [102]
  (*Variation 1*: A woman and a glass are ever in danger.)
  (*Variation 2*: A woman and a glass are never out of danger.)
  Kin, p. 106.
  (1. Brown, p. 110.)
  (2. Whiting, EA, p. 493, W276.)

Women and hens are lost by gadding. [72]
  Hines, p. 292, Pacific Northwest. (Italian)

Women and their wills are dangerous ills. [42]
  Kin, p. 279.

Women and wine are the bane of youth. [72]
  Whiting, EA, p. 494, W284. (1742)

Women and wine, game and deceit, Make the wealth small and the wants great. [72]
  Franklin, 1746.
  Whiting, EA, p. 494, W285.

Women are a good deal like licker, ef you love 'em too hard thar sure to throw you some way. [42]
  Taylor and Whiting, p. 410, #21.

Women are always in extremes. [42]
  (*Variation*: Women are in extremes, they are better or worse than men.)
  Brown, p. 114.
  Kin, p. 281.
  Mieder, Dic., p. 668, #89, Illinois, New York. (1526)
  (Thiselton-Dyer, p. 90.) (French)

Women are ambulating blocks for millinery. [51]
  Mieder, Dic., p. 668, #90, Mississippi.

Women are apt to see chiefly the defects of a man of talent and the merits of a fool. [66]
  Hines, p. 292, Pacific Northwest.

Women are as fickle as April weather. [98]
  Kin, p. 282.
  Mieder, Dic., p. 669, #91, Illinois. (German)

Women are kittle (queer) cattle. [42]
  Whiting, MPPS, p. 695.

Women are like books; too much gilding makes men suspicious that the binding is the most important part. [51]

Mieder, Dic., p. 669, #92.
Women are men with better clothes. [122]
  Sparrow, p. 125.
Women are necessary evils. [86]
  Kin, p. 282.
  Mieder, Dic., p. 669, #93, Illinois. (1547) (Latin)
  Whiting, EA, p. 494, W287.
Women are saints in church, angels in the street, devils in the kitchen, and apes in bed. [42]
  [*See also*: A good wife is a perfect lady in the living room, a good cook in the kitchen, and a harlot in the bedroom.]
  Brown, p. 34.
  Kin, p. 282.
  Mieder, Dic., p. 669, #94, Illinois. (1559)
Women are ships and must be manned. [72]
  Hines, p. 293, Pacific Northwest.
Women are strong when they arm themselves with their weaknesses. [42]
  Kin, p. 282.
  Mieder, Dic., p. 669, #95, Illinois. (1948)
Women are the devil's nets. [42]
  Brown, p. 112.
  Kin, p. 282.
  Mieder, Dic., p. 669, #96, Illinois. (1520)
Women are the root of all evil. [42]
  Mieder, Dic., p. 669, #97, Wisconsin. (1948)
Women are wacky, women are vain; they'd rather be pretty than have a good brain. [51]
  Mieder, Dic., p. 669, #98, New York. (1940)
Women are wise on a sudden, fools on premeditation. [42]
  (*Variation*: Women are wise impromptu, fools on reflection.) (Italian)
  Loomis, GE, p. 197, #30. (1866)
Women at lust are a contradiction. [102]
  Mieder, Dic., p. 669, #99, North Carolina.
Women be forgetful, Children be unkind, Executors are covetous and take what they can find. [42]
  Whiting, MPPS, p. 695.
Women can tolerate everything—except each other. [42]
  Kin, p. 165. [under misogyny]
Women commend an honest man: but they do not like him. [42]
  Brown, p. 114.
Women confess their small faults that their candor may cover great ones. [42]
  Kin, p. 39.
Women, cows, and hens should not run. [73]
  Mieder, Dic., p. 669, #100, North Carolina.

Women distrust men too much in general and not enough in particular. [66]
   Hines, p. 293, Pacific Northwest.
Women do not choose a man because they love him; but because it pleases them to be loved by him. [Alphonse Karr] [66]
   Brown, p. 114.
Women do not read; they listen with the eye. [42]
   Hines, p. 293, Pacific Northwest.
Women forgive injuries but never forget slights. [42]
   Mieder, Dic., p. 669, #101, New York. (1843)
Women grown bad are worse than men, because corruption of the best turns to worst. [78]
   Loomis, GE, p. 197, #24. (1866)
Women have nine measures of talk. [90]
   Yoffie, p. 161, #384. (Yiddish)
Women have no rank. [86]
   Kin, p. 209.
Women have no souls. [42]
   Whiting, EA, p. 494, W288. (1638)
Women have tears at command. [42]
   Whiting, EA, p. 494, W289. (1712)
Women have their fears. [42]
   Mieder, Enc., p. 544, #18028.
   Whiting, EA, p. 494, W290. (1740)
Women in the Senate House are like monkeys in a glass ship. [86]
   Brown, p. 114.
Women laugh when they can and weep when they will. [43]
   (Variation 1: A woman laughs when she can and weeps when she pleases.)
   (Variation 2: A woman laughs when she can but cries whenever she wishes.)
   (Variation 3: Women laugh when they can and cry when they want to.)
   Loomis, GE, p. 197, #32. (1866)
   (1. Brown, p. 112.)
   (2. Mieder, Dic., p. 666, #19, New Jersey.) (1570) (French)
   (3. West, p. 42, Mexican-American.)
Women leave peace behind 'em when they go. [113]
   Mieder, Dic., p. 669, #102, New York. (1906)
Women, like gongs, should be beaten regularly. [86]
   Kin, p. 22.
Women, like princes, find few real friends. [43]
   Hines, p. 293, Pacific Northwest.
Women love men not because they are men but because they are not women. [66]

Kin, p. 165. [under misogyny]
Women must always have the last word. **[43]**
(*Variation 1*: Women will have the last word.)
(*Variation 2*: A woman has the last word.)
Brown, p. 114.
(1. Kin, p. 282.)
(1. Mieder, Dic., p. 669, #104, Illinois, New York.) (1541)
(1. Whiting, EA, p. 494, W291.)
(2. Whiting, MPPS, p. 694.)
Women, priests and poultry are never satisfied. **[73]**
Kin, p. 132.
Women rouge that they may not blush. **[43]**
Kin, p. 221. (Italian)
Women's clocks will walk with every wind. **[98]**
Mieder, Dic., p. 102, #10, North Carolina.
Women's jars breed men's wars. **[51]**
Hines, p. 293, Pacific Northwest. (English)
Kin, p. 135.
Women sometimes exaggerate a little, and this is an important point to
be remembered by men and women. **[43]**
Mieder, Dic., p. 669, #103, Wisconsin.
Women's tongues are made of aspen leaves. **[90]**
Whiting, EA, p. 495, W293. (1747)
Women swallow at one mouthful the lie that flatters and drink drop by
drop the truth that is bitter. **[51]**
Hines, p. 293, Pacific Northwest.
The world is full of wicked women. **[78]**
Mieder, Dic., p. 668, #70, Ohio.
A worthy woman is the crown of her husband. **[30]**
Mieder, Dic., p. 666, #32, New York. (1948)
Would you know your daughter? Then see her in company. **[58]**
Brown, p. 114.
You can never pin a woman down to an answer. **[98]**
Mieder, Dic., p. 669, #106, North Carolina.
You can never tell about women, but if you can, you shouldn't. **[43]**
Mieder, Dic., p. 669, #108.
You cannot pluck roses without fear of thorns nor enjoy a fair wife with-
out danger of horns. **[30]**
Franklin, 1734.
Mieder, Dic., p. 517, #11, Wisconsin.
You can take the girl out of the country, but you can't take the country
out of the girl. **[43]**
(*Variation*: You can take a girl off a farm, but you can't take the farm
out of a girl.)

Mieder, Dic., p. 251, #22, Illinois, Kansas. (original and variation)

You can't keep house with a dead woman. [118]

Mieder, AP, p. 66, Pennsylvania Dutch.

You can't know a girl by her looks or a man by his books. [51]

Kin, p. 12.

You can't live with them (women, men) and you can't live without them.
[43]

Person, p. 182, #225, Washington.

You can't marry a widow, for the widow marries you. [106]

Thompson, p. 484, New York.

You get a woman mad and her blood good and hot, better let her blood
cool for she'll sho' hurt you. [43]

Mieder, Dic., p. 669, #107, South Carolina.

You know a good housekeeper by her windows. [118]

Mieder, TLSM, p. 51, Vermont.

You may know a foolish woman by her finery. [51]

Loomis, GE, p. 197, #27. (1866)

You mustn't rush a lady.

Mieder, Dic., p. 359, #13, Ohio. [43]

A young girl never quite gets over her first man. [66]

[*See also*: A girl's first man (affair) is never forgotten.]

Whiting, PPNC, p. 414, North Carolina.

A young whore, an old saint. [93]

Kin, p. 288.

Mieder, Enc., p. 524, #17305. (English)

A young woman married to an old man must behave like an old woman.
[30]

Kin, p. 288.

Your mother wears combat boots. [56]

Clark, p. 150, #83, North Carolina.

Your own mother wouldn't know you. [56]

Whiting, MPPS, p. 427.

You speak to the daughter, and mean the daughter-in-law. [59]

Yoffie, p. 149, #212. (Spanish, Yiddish)

BIBLIOGRAPHY

WORKS CITED

Books

Adams, Abby, comp. *An Uncommon Scold*. New York: Simon and Schuster, 1989.

Boatwright, Mody C., ed., Wilson M. Hudson and Allen Maxwell, assoc. eds. *Texas Folk and Folklore*. Dallas: Southern Methodist University Press, 1954.

Brown, Raymond Lamont. *A Book of Proverbs*. New York: Taplinger Publishing Company, 1970.

Brunvand, Jan Harold. *A Dictionary of Proverbs and Proverbial Phrases from Books Published by Indiana Authors Before 1890*. Bloomington: Indiana University Press, 1961.

———. *The Study of American Folklore: An Introduction*. 2nd ed. New York: W. W. Norton and Co., Inc., 1978.

Burne, Charlotte Sophia. *The Handbook of Folklore*. London: Sidgwick and Jackson, Ltd., 1914.

Cameron, Deborah. *Feminism and Linguistic Theory*. 1985; New York: St. Martin's Press, 1992.

Coffin, Tristram Potter. *Our Living Traditions: An Introduction to American Folklore*. New York: Basic Books, 1968.

———, and Henning Cohen, eds. *Folklore in America*. Garden City, NY: Doubleday and Co., Inc., 1966.

DeCaro, Francis A., and W. K. McNeil, comps. *American Proverb Literature: A Bibliography*, Bibliographic and Special Series, No. 6. Bloomington, IN: Folklore Forum, 1970.

Dorson, Richard M. *American Folklore*. Chicago: The University of Chicago Press, 1959.

————, ed. *Folklore and Folklife: An Introduction*. Chicago: The University of Chicago Press, 1972.

Dundes, Alan. *Interpreting Folklore*. Bloomington: Indiana University Press, 1980.

Emrich, Duncan. *Folklore on the American Land*. Boston: Little, Brown and Company, 1972.

Fergusson, Rosalind, comp. *The Facts on File Dictionary of Proverbs*. New York: Facts on File Publications, 1983.

Franklin, Benjamin. *Poor Richard's: The Almanacks for the Years 1733–1758*. Edited by Richard Saunders. New York: Heritage Press, 1964.

Hines, Donald M. *Frontier Folksay: Proverbial Lore of the Inland Pacific Northwest Frontier*. N.p.: Norwood Editions, 1977.

Kin, David, ed. *Dictionary of American Proverbs*. New York: New York Philosophical Library, 1955.

Kramar, Cheris. "Folk Linguistics: Wishy-Washy Mommy Talk." In *Exploring Language*, 3rd ed. Edited by Gary Goshgarian. Boston: Little, Boston and Company, 1983.

Kramarae, Cheris. *Women and Men Speaking: Frameworks for Analysis*. Rowley, MA: Newbury House Publishers, Inc., 1981.

Krohn, Kaarle. *Folklore Methodology*. Trans. Roger L. Welsch. Austin: University of Texas Press, 1971.

Lakoff, Robin. "You Are What You Say." In *Exploring Language*, 3rd. ed. Edited by Gary Goshgarian. Boston: Little, Brown and Company, 1983.

McConnell-Ginet, Sally, Ruth Borker, and Nelly Furman, eds. *Women and Language in Literature and Society*. New York: Praeger, 1980.

Mieder, Wolfgang. *American Proverbs: A Study of Texts and Contexts*. New York: Peter Lang, 1989.

————. *Prentice-Hall Encyclopedia of World Proverbs: A Treasury of Wit and Wisdom Through the Ages*. Englewood Cliffs, NJ: Prentice-Hall, 1986.

————. *Talk Less and Say More: Vermont Proverbs*. Shelburne, VT: The New England Press, 1986.

————, ed. in chief, Stewart A. Kingsbury and Kelsie B. Harder, eds. *A Dictionary of American Proverbs*. New York: Oxford University Press, 1992.

Miller, Casey, and Kate Swift. *Words and Women*. Garden City, NY: Anchor Press/Doubleday, 1976.

Norrick, Neal R. *How Proverbs Mean: Semantic Studies in English Proverbs*. New York: Mouton Publishers, 1985.

Smith, Mrs. Morgan, and A. W. Eddins. "Wise Saws from Texas." In *Straight Texas*, a publication of the Texas Folklore Society, no. 13. Hatboro, PA: Folklore Associates, Inc., 1966.

Smith, Philip M. *Language, The Sexes and Society*. New York: Basil Blackwell Inc., 1985.

Taylor, Archer. *The Proverb and an Index to the Proverb*. Hatboro, PA: Folklore Associates, 1962.

————. *Proverbial Comparisons and Similes from California*. Berkeley: University of California Press, 1954.

————, and Bartlett Jere Whiting. *A Dictionary of American Proverbs and Proverbial Phrases, 1820–1880*. Cambridge, MA: The Belknap Press of Harvard University Press, 1958.

Thiselton-Dyer, Thomas Firminger. *Folklore of Women*. Chicago: A. C. McClurg, 1906.

Thompson, Harold W. *Body, Boots and Britches: Folktales, Ballads and Speech from Country New York*. Introduction and Notes by Thomas F. O'Donnell. Syracuse, NY: Syracuse University Press, 1979.

Titelman, Gregory Y. *Popular Proverbs and Sayings*. New York: Gramercy Books, 1997.

Trench, Richard Chenevix. *Proverbs and their Lessons*. New York: E. P. Dutton and Co., 1905. [Previously known as: *On the Lessons in Proverbs*. New York: Blakeman and Mason, 1859.]

Welsch, Roger L. *A Treasury of Nebraska Pioneer Folklore*. Lincoln: University of Nebraska Press, 1941.

West, John O. *Mexican-American Folklore*. Little Rock, AR: August House, 1988.

Whiting, Bartlett Jere. *Early American Proverbs and Proverbial Phrases*. Cambridge, MA: Belknap Press of Harvard University Press, 1977.

———. *Modern Proverbs and Proverbial Sayings*. Cambridge, MA: Harvard University Press, 1989.

———. "Proverbs and Proverbial Sayings." In *The Frank C. Brown Collection of North Carolina Folklore*, vol. 1. Gen. Ed. Newman Ivey White. Durham, NC: Duke University Press, 1952.

Zona, Guy A. *The Soul Would Have No Rainbow If The Eyes Had No Tears*. New York: Simon and Schuster, 1994.

Periodicals

Adams, Owen S. "More California Proverbs." *Western Folklore* 7 (1948): 136–44.

———. "Traditional Proverbs and Sayings from California." *Western Folklore* 6 (1947): 59–64.

Atkinson, Mary J. "Familiar Sayings of Old Time Texans." *Publications of the Texas Folk Lore Society* 5 (1926): 78–92.

Bailey, Larry W., and David Edwards. "Use of Meaningless and Novel Proverbs as a Projective Technique." *Journal of Personality Assessment* 37 (1973): 527–30.

Barbour, Frances M. "Embellishment of the Proverb." *Southern Folklore Quarterly* 28 (1964): 291–98.

Bradley, F. W. "South Carolina Proverbs." *Southern Folklore Quarterly* 1 (1937): 57–101.

Brewster, Paul G. "Folk Sayings from Indiana." *American Speech* 14 (1939): 261–68.

———. "Still Another Batch of Indiana Sayings." *American Speech* 19 (1944): 155–56.

Clark, Joseph D. "Proverbs and Sayings from North Carolina." *Southern Folklore Quarterly* 26 (1962): 145–73.

Dion, Kenneth L. "Psychology and Proverbs." *Canadian Psychology* 31.3 (1990): 209–11.

Farrer, Claire R. "Women and Folklore: Images and Genres." *Journal of American Folklore* 88 (Jan.-March 1975): v–xv; reissued, Prospect Heights, IL: Waveland Press, Inc., 1986.

Gorham, Donald R. "A Proverbs Test for Clinical and Experimental Use." *Psychological Reports* 2 (1956): 1–12. (Monograph Supplement 1)

Hardie, Margaret. "Proverbs and Proverbial Expressions Current in the United States East of the Missouri and North of the Ohio Rivers." *American Speech* 4 (1928–29): 461–72.

Hendricks, George D. "Texas Folk Proverbs." *Western Folklore* 21 (1962): 92.

Hertzler, Joyce. "The Social Wisdom of the Primitives with Special Reference to Their Proverbs." *Social Forces* 11 (1933): 313–25.

Hoffman, W. J. "Folklore of the Pennsylvania Germans." *Journal of American Folklore* 2 (1889): 191–202.

"Indian Proverbs." *Journal of American Folklore* 19 (1906): 173.

Loomis, C. Grant. "Proverbs in the Farmer's Almanac(k)." *Western Folklore* 15 (1956): 172–78.

———. "Proverbs in the Golden Era." *Western Folklore* 14 (1955): 196–99.

Mason, Diane. "Quiet Strength Shakes Earth." *Beaumont Enterprise* 5 July 1991: 3B.

Mieder, Wolfgang. "Proverbs of the Native Americans." *Western Folklore* 48.4 (1989): 256–60.

Pearce, T. M. "The English Proverb in New Mexico." *Western Folklore* 5 (1946): 350–54.

Penfield, Joyce, and Mary Duru. "Proverbs: Metaphors That Teach." *Anthropological Quarterly* 61.3 (1988): 119–28.

Person, Henry A. "Proverbs and Proverbial Lore from the State of Washington." *Western Folklore* 17 (1958): 176–85.

Raymond, Joseph. "Tension in Proverbs: More Light on International Understanding." *Western Folklore* 15 (1956): 153–58.

Seitel, Peter. "Proverbs: A Social Use of Metaphor." *Genre* 2 (1969): 143–61.

Sparrow. "Proverbs." *Whole Earth Review* 63 (1989): 124–25.

Storm, Hiroko. "Women in Japanese Proverbs." *Asian Folklore Studies* 51.2 (1992): 167–82.

Taylor, Archer. "Problems in the Study of Proverbs." *Journal of American Folklore* 47 (1934): 1–21.

———.. "The Wisdom of Many and Wit of One." *Swarthmore College Bulletin* 54 (1962): 4–7.

Yoffie, Leah Rachel. "Yiddish Proverbs, Sayings, Etc. in St. Louis, Missouri." *Journal of American Folklore* 33 (1920): 134–65.

WORKS CONSULTED

Books

Apperson, G. L. *English Proverbs and Proverbial Phrases: A Historical Dictionary*. New York: E. P. Dutton and Company, Inc., 1929.

Bailey, Nathan. *Divers Proverbs*. New Haven, CT: Yale University Press, 1917.

———. *Old English Proverbs*. Metuchen, NJ: Scarecrow Press, 1992.

Barbour, Frances M., ed. *Proverbs and Proverbial Phrases of Illinois*. Carbondale: Southern Illinois University Press, 1965.

Beilenson, Evelyn L., and Ann Tenenbaum, eds. *Wit and Wisdom of Famous American Women*. White Plains, NY: Peter Pauper Press, Inc., 1986.

Ben-Amos, Dan, ed. *Folklore Genres*. Austin: University of Texas Press, 1976.

Blackwood, Margaret. *The Monstrous Regiment: A Book of Aphorisms*. London: Andre Deutsch, 1990.

Blue, John S. *Hoosier Tales and Proverbs*. Dexter, MI: Thomson-Shore, Inc., 1982.

Bluestein, Gene. *The Voice of the Folk: Folklore and Literary Theory*. Amherst: University of Massachusetts Press, 1972.

Bohn, Henry G. *A Handbook of Proverbs*. London: H. G. Bohn, 1855; rpt., New York: AMS Press, 1968.

———. *A Polyglot of Foreign Proverbs*. London: H. G. Bohn, 1857; rpt., New York: AMS Press, 1968.

Bonser, Wilfred, ed., and T. A. Stephens, comp. *Proverb Literature: A Bibliography of Works Relating to Proverbs*. London: William Glaisher, Ltd., 1930.

Botkin, Benjamin Albert. *Folk-say: A Regional Miscellany*. Norman: University of Oklahoma Press, 1930.

———. *Sidewalks of America*. New York: Bobbs-Merrill Company, Inc., 1954.

———. *A Treasury of New England Folklore*. New York: Crown, 1947.

———. *A Treasury of Southern Folklore*. New York: Crown, 1949.

Bratcher, James T. *An Analytical Index to Publications of the Texas Folklore Society*, Vols. 1–36. Dallas: Southern Methodist University Press, 1973.

Bryant, Margaret M. *Proverbs and How to Collect Them*. Greensboro, NC: American Dialect Society, 1945.

Cheales, Alan B. *Proverbial Folklore*, 2nd ed. London: Folcroft Library Eds., 1976.

Christy, Robert. *Proverbs, Maxims and Phrases for All Ages*. New York: G. P. Putnam and Sons, 1888.

Cobos, Ruben. *Refranes: Southwestern Spanish Proverbs*. Santa Fe: Museum of New Mexico Press, 1985.

Collis, Harry. *101 American English Proverbs: Understanding Language and Culture through Commonly Used Sayings*. Lincolnwood, IL: Passport Books, 1992.

Davidson, Levette Jay. *A Guide to American Folklore*. Denver: University of Denver Press, 1951.

DeCaro, Francis A. "Riddles and Proverbs." In *Folk Groups and Folklore Genres*. Edited by Elliott Oring. Logan: Utah State University Press, 1986.

———. *Women and Folklore: A Bibliographic Survey*. Westport, CT: Greenwood Press, 1983.

Dobie, J. Frank. *Spur-of-the-Cock*. Austin: Texas Folklore Society, 1933; Facsimile Edition, Dallas: Southern Methodist University Press, 1965.

Dorson, Richard M. *Folklore and Fakelore: Essays Toward a Discipline of Folk Studies*. Cambridge, MA: Harvard University Press, 1976.

Dundes, Alan. *Folklore Theses and Dissertations in the United States*. Austin: University of Texas Press, 1976.

———. *The Study of Folklore*. Englewood Cliffs, NJ: Prentice-Hall, Inc., 1965.

Glazer, Mark, comp. *A Dictionary of Mexican American Proverbs*. New York: Greenwood Press, 1987.

———, ed. *Flour from Another Sack*. Edinburg, TX: Pan American University, 1982.

Goldstein, Kenneth S. *A Guide for Field Workers in Folklore*. Hatboro, PA: Folklore Associates, Inc., 1964.

Haywood, Charles. *A Bibliography of North American Folklore and Folksong*. New York: Greenberg, 1951.

Hollis, Susan Tower, Linda Pershing, and M. Jane Young. *Feminist Theory and the Study of Folklore*. Urbana: University of Illinois Press, 1993.

Honeck, Richard P., and Robert R. Hoffman, eds. *Cognition and Figurative Language*. Hillsdale, NJ: Lawrence Erlbaum Associates, 1980.

Hulme, Frederick Edward. *Proverb Lore*. Detroit: Gale Research Company, 1968.

Johnson, Clifton. *What They Say in New England, and Other American Folklore*. New York: Columbia University Press, 1963.

Jordan, Rosan A. *The Folklore and Ethnic Identity of a Mexican-American Woman*. Doctoral Dissertation, Indiana University, 1975.

——, and Susan J. Kalcik, eds. *Women's Folklore, Women's Culture*. Philadelphia: University of Pennsylvania Press, 1985.

Katz, Elaine S. *Folklore for the Time of Your Life*. Birmingham, AL: Oxmoor House, Inc., 1978.

Koch, William E. *Folklore from Kansas: Customs, Beliefs and Superstitions*. Lawrence, KS: The Regents Press of Kansas, 1980.

Krappe, Alexander H. *The Science of Folklore*. London: n.p., 1930; reprint New York: W. W. Norton, 1964.

Kremer, Edmund P. *German Proverbs and Proverbial Phrases with Their English Counterparts*. Stanford, CA: Stanford University Press, 1955.

Lakoff, Robin. *Language and Woman's Place*. New York: Harper, 1975.

Leach, Maria, ed. *Standard Dictionary of Folklore, Mythology and Legend*. 2 vols. New York: Funk and Wagnalls Company, 1949, 1950.

Marett, Robert Ranulph. *Psychology and Folk-lore*. London: Methuen and Co., Ltd., 1920.

Mieder, Wolfgang. *As Sweet As Apple Cider: Vermont Expressions*. Shelburne, VT: The New England Press, 1988.

——. *International Proverb Scholarship: An Annotated Bibliography*. New York: Garland, 1990.

——. *Investigations of Proverbs, Proverbial Expressions, Quotations and Cliches*. New York: Peter Lang, 1984.

——. *Proverbs Are Never Out of Season: Popular Wisdom in the Modern Age*. New York: Oxford University Press, 1993.

——. *Wise Words: Essays on the Proverb*. New York: Garland Publishing, Inc., 1994.

——, and Alan Dundes, eds. *The Wisdom of Many: Essays on the Proverb*. Madison: University of Wisconsin Press, 1994.

Mingo, Jack, and John Javna. *Primetime Proverbs: The Book of TV Quotes*. New York: Harmony Books, 1989.

Nilsen, Alleen Pace, Haig Bosmajian, H. Lee Gershung, and Julia P. Stanley. *Sexism and Language*. Urbana, IL: National Council of Teachers of English, 1977.

Patterson, Daniel W., ed. *Folklore Studies in Honor of Arthur Palmer Hudson*. Chapel Hill: The North Carolina Folklore Society, 1965.

Pearson, Judy C. *Gender and Communication*. Dubuque, IA: William C. Brown, 1991.

———. *Interpersonal Communication: Clarity, Confidence, Concern*. Glenview, IL: Scott and Foresman, 1982.

Phipps, Etienne Juarez. *Women's Folklore and Health Care: Traditions at Work*. Doctoral Dissertation, University of Pennsylvania, 1980.

Pullar-Strecker, H. *Proverbs for Pleasure*. New York: Philosophical Library, 1955.

Radner, Joan Newlon, ed. *Feminist Messages: Coding in Women's Folk Culture*. Urbana: University of Illinois Press, 1993.

Randolph, Vance. *Ozark Folklore: A Bibliography*. Bloomington: Indiana University Research Center for the Language Sciences, 1972.

———, and George P. Wilson. *Down in the Holler: A Gallery of Ozark Folk Speech*. Norman: University of Oklahoma Press, 1953.

Simmons, Merle Edwin. *Folklore Bibliography for 1975*. Philadelphia: Institute for the Study of Human Issues, 1979.

———. *Folklore Bibliography for 1976*. Philadelphia: Institute for the Study of Human Issues, 1981.

Slung, Michele. *Momilies: As My Mother Used to Say*. New York: Ballantine Books, 1985.

Smith, William George. *Oxford Dictionary of English Proverbs*. Oxford: The Clarendon Press, 1948.

Stevenson, Burton Egbert. *The Home Book of Proverbs, Maxims and Familiar Phrases*. New York: Macmillan, 1948.

Tallman, Marjorie. *Dictionary of American Folklore*. New York: Philosophical Library, 1959.

Tannen, Deborah. *Gender and Discourse*. New York: Oxford University Press, 1994.

———. *Talking from 9 to 5: How Women's and Men's Conversational Styles Affect Who Gets Heard, Who Gets Credit, and What Gets Done at Work*. New York: W. Morrow, 1994.

———. *You Just Don't Understand: Women and Men in Conversation*. New York: W. Morrow, 1990.

———, ed. *Framing in Discourse*. New York: Oxford University Press, 1993.

———, ed. *Gender and Conversational Interaction*. New York: Oxford University Press, 1993.

———, and Muriel Saville-Troike, eds. *Perspectives on Silence*. Norwood, NJ: Ablex Publishing Corporation, 1985.

Thorne, Barrie, Cheris Kramarae, and Nancy Henley. *Language, Gender and Society*. Rowley, MA: Newbury House Publishers, Inc., 1983.

Tilley, Morris P. *A Dictionary of the Proverbs in England in the Sixteenth and Seventeenth Centuries: A Collection of the Proverbs in English Literature and the Dictionaries of the Period*. Ann Arbor: University of Michigan Press, 1950.

Tupper, Martin Farquhar. *Proverbial Philosophy*. New York: George A. Leavitt, 1852.

White, Newman Ivey. *The Frank C. Brown Collection of North Carolina Folklore*. Vol. 1. Durham, NC: Duke University Press, 1952.

Woods, Ralph L., ed. *A Treasury of the Familiar*. Foreword by John Kieran. New York: The Macmillan Company, 1943.

Periodicals

Adams, Owen S. "Proverbial Comparisons from California." *Western Folklore* 5 (1946): 334–38.

———. "Proverbial Phrases from California." *Western Folklore* 8 (1949): 95–116.

Allison, Robert E., and A. L. Minkes. "Principles, Proverbs, and Shibboleths of Administration." *International Journal of Technology Management* 5.2 (1990): 179–87.

Arewa, E. Ojo, and Alan Dundes. "Proverbs and the Ethnography of Speaking." *American Anthropologist* 66 (1964): no. 6, part 2: 70–85.

Barrick, Mac E. "Early Proverbs From Carlisle, Pennsylvania. (1788–1820)." *Kentucky Folklore Quarterly* 13 (1968): 193–217.

Barrick, Max F. "Ruxton's Western Proverbs." *Western Folklore* 34 (July 1975): 215–25.

Bass, Bernard. "Validity Studies of a Proverbs Personality Test." *Journal of Applied Psychology* 41 (1957): 158–60.

Baughman, Ernest W. "Rhymes and Sayings." *New Mexico Folklore Record* 6 (1951–1952): 23–25.

Benjafield, John. "Imagery, Concreteness, Goodness, and Familiarity Ratings for 500 Proverbs Sampled from the *Oxford Dictionary of English Proverbs*." *Behavior Research Methods, Instruments and Computers* 25.1 (1993): 27–40.

Blair, Marion E. "The Prevalence of Older English Proverbs in Blount County, Tennessee." *Tennessee Folklore Society Bulletin* 4 (1938): 1–24.

Boswell, George. "Folk Wisdom in Northeast Kentucky." *Tennessee Folklore Society Bulletin* 33 (1967): 10–17.

Brewster, Paul G. "More Indiana Sayings." *American Speech* 16 (1941): 21–25.

"California Proverbs." *Western Folklore* 3 (1944): 232.

"California Proverbs and Sententious Sayings." *Western Folklore* 10 (1951): 248–49.

Chamberlain, Alexander. "Proverbs in the Making." *Journal of American Folklore* 17 (1904): 161–70, 268–78.

Clark, J. D. "Similes from the Folk Speech of the South: A Supplement to Wilstach's Compilation." *Southern Folklore Quarterly* 4 (1940): 205–26.

Collins, Camilla A., ed. "Folklore Fieldwork: Sex, Sexuality, and Gender." *Southern Folklore* 47.1 (1990): 1–99.

Cox, Ernest. "Rustic Imagery in Mississippi Proverbs." *Southern Folklore Quarterly* 11 (1947): 263–67.

Davidson, Levette Jay. "Westernisms." *American Speech* 17 (1942): 72–73.

deBonis, Monique, Catherine Epelbaum, and Andre Feline. "Cognitive Processing of Contradictory Statements: An Experimental Study of Reasoning on Proverbs in Schizophrenia." *Psychopathology* 25.2 (1992): 100–108.

Doctor, Raymond D. "Indian Enumerative Proverbs." *Proverbium* 10 (1993): 51–64.

Dundes, Alan. "On the Structure of the Proverb." *Proverbium* 25 (1975): 961–73.

Folsom, Steven. "Proverbs in Recent American Country Music." *Proverbium* 10 (1993): 65–88.

Gorham, Donald R. "Use of the Proverbs Test for Differentiating Schizophrenics from Normals." *Journal of Consulting Psychology* 20 (1956): 435–40.

Halpert, Herbert. "More Proverbial Comparisons from West Tennessee." *Tennessee Folklore Society Bulletin* 18 (1952): 15–21.

———. "Proverbial Comparisons from West Tennessee." *Tennessee Folklore Society Bulletin* 17 (1951): 49–61.

Haynes, Rita M. "Proverb Familiarity and the Mental Status Examination." *Bulletin of the Menninger Clinic* 57.4 (1993): 523–28.

Honeck, Richard P. "Proverbs: The Extended Conceptual Base and Great Chain Metaphor Theories." *Metaphor and Symbolic Activity* 9.2 (1994): 85–112.

Hughes, Muriel J. "Vermont Proverbial Comparisons and Similes." *Vermont History* 26 (1958): 257–93.

———. "Vermont Proverbs and Proverbial Sayings." *Vermont History* 28 (1960): 113–42, 200–230.

Jente, Richard. "The American Proverb." *American Speech* 7 (1931–32): 342–48.

Kauffman, Draper. "System Proverbs." *Et cetera* 47.1 (Spring 1990): 20–29.

Kemper, Susan. "Comprehension and the Interpretation of Proverbs." *Journal of Psycholinguistic Research* 10 (1981): 179–98.

Kirshenblatt-Gimblett, Barbara. "Toward a Theory of Proverb Meaning." *Proverbium* 22 (1973): 821–27.

Kuhel, Pat. "Lebanese-American Proverbs and Proverbial Lore." *Mid-America Folklore* 19.2 (Fall 1991): 110–17.

Lewis, Mary Ellen B. "The Feminists Have Done It: Applied Folklore." *Journal of American Folklore* 87 (1974): 85–87.

Loeb, Edwin. "The Function of Proverbs in the Intellectual Development of Primitive Peoples." *Scientific Monthly* 74 (1952): 100–104.

Lundberg, George A. "The Semantics of Proverbs." *ETC: A Review of General Semantics* 15 (1958): 215–17.

McNeil, W. K. "Folklore from Big Flat, Arkansas, III: Proverbs and Proverbial Phrases." *Mid-America Folklore* 12.2 (1984): 27–30.

———. "Proverbs Used in New York Autograph Albums 1820–1900." *Southern Folklore Quarterly* 33 (1969): 352–59.

Messenger, John. "Peasants, Proverbs, and Projection." *Central Issues in Anthropology* 9 (April 1, 1991): 99.

Mieder, Wolfgang. "American Literature: A Bibliography; Review." *Journal of American Folklore* 87 (1974): 374–76.

———. "Good Proverbs Make Good Vermonters." *Proverbium* 9 (1992): 159–77.

———. "The Proverb and Anglo-American Literature." *Southern Folklore Quarterly* 38 (1974): 49–62.

———. "The Use of Proverbs in Psychological Testing." *Journal of the Folklore Institute* 15 (1978): 45–55.

Needham, Gwendolyn B. "New Light on Maids' 'Leading Apes in Hell.' " *Journal of American Folklore* 75 (1962): 106–19.

Newell, W. W. "Proverbs and Phrases." *Journal of American Folklore* 2 (1889): 153–54.

Nguyen, Nguyen. "Proverbs as Psychological Interpretations among Vietnamese." *Asian Folklore Studies* 50.2 (1991): 311–18.

Norrick, Neal R. "Proverbial Emotions." *Proverbium* 11 (1994): 207–15.

Odell, Ruth. "Nebraska Smart Sayings." *Southern Folklore Quarterly* 12 (1948): 185–95.

Pearce, Helen. "Folk Sayings in a Pioneer Family of Western Oregon." *Western Folklore* 5 (1946): 229–42.

Richardson, Claudia, and Joseph A. Church. "A Developmental Analysis of Proverb Interpretation." *Journal of Genetic Psychology* 94 (1959): 169–79.

Rogers, Tim B. "Proverbs as Psychological Theories." *Canadian Psychology* 31.3 (1990): 195–207.

Sackett, S. J. "Poetry and Folklore: Some Points of Affinity." *Journal of American Folklore* 77 (1964): 143–53.

Taft, Michael. "Proverbs in the Blues: How Frequent Is Frequent?" *Proverbium* 11 (1994): 227–58.

Taylor, Archer. "An Introductory Bibliography for the Study of Proverbs." *Modern Philology* 30 (1932): 195–210.

———. "Investigation of English Proverbs, Proverbial and Conventional Phrases, Oaths and Cliches." *Journal of American Folklore* 65 (1952): 255–65.

———. "No House is Big Enough for Two Women." *Western Folklore* 16 (1957): 121–24.

Temple, Jon G. "Literal vs. Nonliteral Reminders for Proverbs." *Bulletin of the Psychonomic Society* 30.1 (1992): 67.

Thompson, Harold W. "Proverbs and Sayings." *New York Folklore Quarterly* 5 (1949): 230–35, 296–300.

Thurston, H. S. "Sayings and Proverbs from Massachusetts." *Journal of American Folklore* 19 (1906): 122.

Tidwell, James N. "Adam's Off Ox: A Study in the Exactness of the Inexact." *Journal of American Folklore* 66 (1953): 291–94.

Whiting, Bartlett Jere. "The Nature of the Proverb." *Harvard University Studies and Notes in Philology and Literature* 14 (1932): 273–307.

———. "The Origin of the Proverb." *Harvard University Studies and Notes in Philology and Literature* 13 (1931): 47–80.

———. "Proverbial Sayings from Fisher's River, North Carolina." *Southern Folklore Quarterly* 11 (1947): 173–85.

———. "Sayings from Fisher's River." *Journal of American Folklore* 47 (1934): 22–44.

Williamson, Julia. "A Culture Capsule that Works." *TESOL Journal* 1.2 (1991): 32.

Wolkomir, Richard. "A Proverb Each Day Keeps This Scholar at Play." *Smithsonian* 23.6 (1992): 110–18.

Yates, Irene. "A Collection of Proverbs and Proverbial Sayings from South Carolina Literature." *Journal of American Folklore* 11 (1947): 187–99.

Index

About the Author

LOIS KERSCHEN was Director of Continuing Education at Frank Phillips College. She previously taught at Texas Tech University and was the Associate Director of Graduate Studies and Research at Lamar University.